TRUE TO YOU

ALSO BY DR. KATHLEEN SMITH

Everything Isn't Terrible:
Conquer Your Insecurities, Interrupt Your Anxiety,
and Finally Calm Down

TRUE
TO YOU

A Therapist's Guide to Stop Pleasing
Others and Start Being Yourself

DR. KATHLEEN SMITH

Copyright © 2024 Annie Kathleen Smith

The right of Annie Kathleen Smith to be identified as the Author of the Work has been asserted by her in accordance with the Copyright, Designs and Patents Act 1988.

Originally published in the USA in 2024 by St. Martin's Essentials, an imprint of St. Martin's Publishing Group

First published in Great Britain in 2024 by Headline Home, an imprint of Headline Publishing Group

5

Cataloguing in Publication Data is available from the British Library

Trade paperback ISBN 978 1 0354 1754 4
eISBN 978 1 0354 1755 1

Cover design by D. Soleil Paz

Printed and bound in Great Britain by Clays Ltd, Elcograf S.p.A.

Headline's policy is to use papers that are natural, renewable and recyclable products and made from wood grown in well-managed forests and other controlled sources. The logging and manufacturing processes are expected to conform to the environmental regulations of the country of origin.

HEADLINE PUBLISHING GROUP
An Hachette UK Company
Carmelite House
50 Victoria Embankment
London EC4Y 0DZ

The authorised representative in the EEA is Hachette Ireland, 8 Castlecourt Centre, Dublin 15, D15 XTP3, Ireland (email: info@hbgi.ie)

www.headline.co.uk
www.hachette.co.uk

For my daughter, who knows how to be herself

CONTENTS

TRUE TO YOU

INTRODUCTION

HUMANS ARE MASTER pretenders. At first glance, most of us seem stronger, calmer, and more mature than we really are. When people applaud our accomplishments, it's easy to look confident. If we love to control others, we can seem so helpful. When our brains are buzzing with expert advice, we look pretty damn smart.

Look closely, and you'll start to see the cracks. To be human is to have gaping holes in your own maturity, the doubts and weaknesses that you've patched over with praise from a boss, help from your partner, or reassurance from a friend when a date doesn't text back. What we don't have we tend to borrow from others.

We borrow because we are deeply social creatures. We were built for relationships. Our brains are designed to read the room and to follow the group. To experience distress in others as if it were our own. Humans have an enormous capacity, more than any other creature, to guess what other people are thinking about them. This deep focus on others, the pull toward cooperating and keeping people happy, is one of our greatest evolutionary gifts. It is the glue that binds families, friends, organizations, and communities. But sometimes, a superpower can feel like a curse.

We're so good at reading others, sometimes we forget to know ourselves. We can think and act as individuals by adopting different beliefs or moving in a new direction. People can hop off their hamster wheels. They can learn to disappoint people. They can say to their family, "This is who I am. This is what I believe." They can be themselves without giving in to, or giving up on, important relationships.

In times of stress, however, it's so hard to hold on to yourself. Our individuality tends to get lost in the togetherness. We treat our relationships like a giant marketplace, borrowing and lending calmness, capabilities, or quick solutions with those around us. This is why it feels natural to take advice from your friends when you're second-guessing a career decision. Why you can't help but take over when your spouse loads the dishwasher like a confused raccoon. Anxiety blurs the lines between our responsibilities and others', between our thinking and others'.

The more "self" you borrow from others, the more your functioning depends on keeping other people calm and happy. This is how life becomes a roller coaster ride. You ride the highs when someone pats you on the head or lets you run the show. But on the days when no one cooperates, or acknowledges you, you might nosedive into despair and self-criticism.

When you spend your energy trying to be what other people want you to be (or trying to get other people to be what you want them to be), four very predictable things are going to happen to you:

1. You'll have no energy left to pursue what's important to you.
2. You'll become more allergic to any distress in your relationships.
3. You'll become more responsible for others than for yourself.
4. You'll abandon your beliefs the second anyone disapproves of them.

This is the perfect recipe for burnout—the type of burnout we try to cure with constant content consumption. We seek fast and easy solutions, using the certainty of others to relieve our own anxieties. But we can't save ourselves with more borrowing. We have to start building something new. Something that feels truer to ourselves.

WHAT'S BOWEN THEORY?

To be a human is to live with the reality of those two essential, often competing forces—the drives to connect with others and to direct ourselves as individuals. It's the wonderful dance of being a person. We cannot be true to ourselves by going it alone or by always going with the group. We need one another, and we need a self.

The trouble is, we don't have much of either these days. We're more disconnected than ever, having less time for family, friends, and our communities. And we live in an anxious world, uncertain of what's real on the internet, what's next in the parade of global crises, or what's really needed from us to solve these big problems. No wonder we're so quick to grab on to the latest guru. Why we settle our fears with self-help content that has little self in it at all. We borrow answers, beliefs, and values that feel "good enough," because we're too exhausted to know our own minds. Perhaps rather than answers, we need better questions. A different way of thinking about human behavior.

As a therapist, I use a theory known as Bowen family systems theory, or Bowen theory for short. Murray Bowen was an American psychiatrist and researcher who wanted to understand how some families coped better with challenges than others. Why did some families put more pressure on one another to be a certain way, while others allowed family members to function a little more as individuals? In the 1950s, Bowen led a historic study at the National Institute of Mental Health (NIMH) that involved housing entire families on a research ward to observe their relationships. Using these observations, Bowen developed a theory of human behavior to explain how some people end up with more emotional maturity (a variable he called "differentiation of self") than others.

Many of Bowen's psychoanalytic predecessors had treated humans as special, almost mystical creatures. But Bowen saw humans as products of evolution. He believed that human behavior was heavily influenced by the processes that governed the natural world. That families were natural systems, trying their best to survive and thrive. Therefore, we can learn something about ourselves by studying other systems, whether it's a troop of chimpanzees, a colony of ants, or a forest of trees.

Bowen observed what could happen when a person began to look at their relationship systems as natural systems. To see behavioral patterns as adaptive rather than dysfunctional. People began to gain a kind of emotional objectivity about how the family functioned. They stopped blaming people and became more curious about relationship patterns. And they started to change their part in these patterns. In other words, they were able to become more of a self in the system. They weren't doomed to forever repeat the multigenerational patterns in their families.

Bowen worked with people who wanted to increase their level of maturity in adulthood. People who wanted to be more responsible for themselves and less caught up in automatic, reactive patterns of the group. He developed a training program to help people apply this thinking to their lives and work. I have had the privilege of studying and teaching in one of these programs, years after Bowen's death.

There are some significant differences between psychotherapy using a system-focused lens (used in Bowen theory) and psychotherapy that takes an individual focus. To start, Bowen theorized that growth didn't happen primarily through the therapeutic relationship (clinician and client), but through learning to represent ourselves in our most challenging relationships. He thought that problems created by relationship systems could be fixed within those relationship systems. Growing up is a process of differentiating one's self in important relationships, by defining your own thinking and holding on to it in an anxious system. By building a more solid self, a person learns to direct their life more by their beliefs and principles, and less by the patterns a system activates to keep things calm. Patterns like distancing, constant fighting, overfunctioning and underfunctioning, or anxiously focusing on a kid.

What I appreciate about Bowen theory is that it is more focused on the "how" than the "what" in our choices. It doesn't tell people what to think, but it teaches people how to think about human behavior. "What should I do?" is a useful question. "How do I make decisions?" is even more useful. How do you decide what's best for you? How do you measure what a good day or good work looks like? Does it look like borrowing the most convenient definitions from the internet or your friends, or does it look like defining your best thinking? Google can certainly play a role, but so can your own damn prefrontal cortex.

Bowen also observed that when a person became more responsible for themselves, they became "less irresponsibly overinvolved with others." This overinvolvement, the drive to control how other people react to you or how they live their lives, eats up so much of our energy. But growing up requires no cooperation from others. Fixing your family doesn't teach you how to live with them. Gaining your mother's or your boss's approval doesn't make you more mature. Little by little, you can recapture energy you put into people pleasing, avoiding conflict, or managing others, and redirect it toward building a more thoughtful life and more fulfilling relationships. You can step back and see how your partner is more capable than you realized. You can tell a friend what you believe rather than what she wants to hear. By being truer to ourselves, we create opportunities for others to do the same.

This sounds so nice, so there must be a catch, right? The catch is that a relationship system isn't easily changed. It has a vested interest in keeping things calm and predictable, in pressuring you to go along with the group or tossing you out of it. In other words, people clap back. They will have lots of opinions about what you're doing. They will tell you whether you have room for dessert, or another graduate degree, or a boyfriend who makes his own knitwear. They'll expect you to calm them down, adopt their beliefs, or sit down and just be quiet. If you don't, they might insult you, stop speaking to you, or make you trend on social media.

These are the challenges where the self can shrink into submission, or it can step forward and learn to dance. You can build the emotional courage needed to live out your principles, but also live in relationship to other humans. You can be responsible for yourself, and let others do the same. Is this a lifelong endeavor? Absolutely. But over time, we can teach our brains that distress, disagreement, and disapproval are not just survivable—they are the crucible where we fashion who we are.

HOW THE BOOK WORKS

True to You is a book for people who are masters at reading others, but struggle to know themselves. For people who please others to feel steady, or realize their relationships are stuck in superficial chitchat. If you'd like to stop letting people's real or imaginary reactions dictate your beliefs, your values, or even what shoes you put on before you walk out the door, then keep reading.

Each chapter of the book will tell the story of a person's efforts to become more of a self in their relationships. These stories are composites of my therapy clients (with identifying details changed to protect confidentiality). I'll tell the story of Sylvie, a young woman who struggles to build deeper relationships with her friends and family. And Luis, a constant consumer of motivational content who wants to learn to trust himself. You'll meet Julian, who starts to shake off some of his need to impress others. And Naima, who's trying to stop overfunctioning for her husband. In these thirteen stories, you'll meet people who began to observe their automatic reactions and be less driven by them. People who started to enjoy their relationships because they put less pressure on them.

The book is divided into two parts. The first part describes the predictable, universal patterns that relationship systems use to manage anxiety. The convenient ways we keep things calm, and how we sacrifice ourselves (and others) in the process. The second part of the book explores what it can look like to turn off our factory settings and begin to direct ourselves as individuals. To have richer relationships because we are operating with a little more self. At the end of each chapter, you'll find exercises that I encourage you to complete. Keeping a record of your own best thinking will be more helpful than any answer I could give you.

My hope is that by reading this book, you can learn to take a systems focus to everyday life. Because our big brains evolved to navigate complex social systems, we cannot discount their influence on our lives. Yet our current culture takes an individualistic, symptom-based approach to mental health. We are very focused on how our bodies and brains manage stress, for good reasons. But we must also consider how the groups to which we belong (e.g. families, communities, countries) manage stress. When we observe ourselves in a vacuum, we miss out on what these emotional systems can teach us.

So as you read this book, I encourage you to try out this different lens for thinking about human behavior, setting the individual focus aside for a bit. Zoom out with me, seeing yourself as a part of many natural systems, what Bowen called emotional systems. These systems could be your family or work team, your congregation or your classroom, your book club or your baseball team. Each system is trying its best to keep things calm through predictable, universal patterns. And you can't really know yourself without understanding how the emotional system functions.

Bowen theory encourages its students to take a researcher's attitude to life. To stand at the top of the stadium, or sit at the end of the dinner table, and see what people do when you dial up the stress. Through observation, we find opportunities to interrupt what's automatic. Opportunities to fill the gaps in our own maturity and live a life that isn't just about keeping everybody happy. Bowen described this as the move from our pretend self, or pseudo-self, to a more solid one.

When you're working on building a more solid self, you have to figure out what you actually think and believe when facing life's challenges. You learn to be a mind knower rather than just a mind reader. You create operating instructions that light the way on dark days. And you learn to embrace the anxiety that comes with living from the inside out. This work doesn't make us less relational creatures. In fact, it paves the way to more rewarding relationships with our fellow humans.

If you want to start growing up, you have to build from the ground up. Throw away that paintbrush and grab a shovel because it's time to stop painting the trim and start digging up the foundation. Who are you now, and who could you be? Let's find out.

PART I

THE RELATIONSHIP PATTERNS THAT KEEP US STUCK

1

HOW WE LOSE OURSELVES

"Taking on a challenge is a lot like riding a horse, isn't it? If you're comfortable while you're doing it, you're probably doing it wrong."
—Ted Lasso, *Ted Lasso*

MARIE'S LIFE WAS like a closet full of clothes that didn't quite fit. New to Washington, DC, the twenty-eight-year-old spent her days working as a fundraiser for her mother's alma mater. At night she barhopped with her boyfriend's law school buddies, or dodged fly balls on his softball team. Her schedule was full, but her life wasn't. She'd gone to several therapists over the years, eager to follow their instructions. They sent her to Al-Anon to help her deal with her father's history of substance use. They printed worksheets to help keep her anxious thoughts at bay. Everything helped, until it didn't.

Marie was a likable person. Small talk came easily to her, and she was quick to mimic body language. Not in a manipulative way—it was just the mark of a woman who wanted to make everyone around her feel comfortable. Her laser focus on others was a useful skill for her fundraising job, but it generated tension in her romantic life. Her boyfriend, Jake, was a frazzled law student with a full social calendar.

So after a full day of work, Marie dragged herself to softball games, networking nights, and lecture series so she could see him. Borrowing her boyfriend's friend group was less intimidating than building her own in a new city.

When Marie grew tired of borrowing Jake's routine, the conflict started. She demanded that Jake cut back on his socializing and spend more time with her. When he refused, she kept showing up at the grad school gatherings. *It's better than nothing,* she told herself.

Most people would say that their life choices don't fit them perfectly. We're a mishmash of beliefs and values we've borrowed from people who are important to us. A combination of choices that seem to get us some love and attention. This is because we look to others to find ourselves. When experts give us answers, we take them. When your friends get Botox, it begins to feel necessary. When you just want to survive another Easter dinner with your family, you accept that Jesus rose from the dead and pass the mashed potatoes. The decisions themselves aren't the problem. It's how quickly we adopt them into our lives. Do you stop to think? Or do you toss them into your shopping cart and say, "Good enough"?

We borrow from others because we are social creatures. We care a lot about what other people think about us and how they will react to us. We'd like to avoid disagreement, disapproval, and rejection as much as possible. Because deep in our brain is a very ancient fear, the worst thing that can happen to a social mammal: being tossed out of the group.

Being part of a relationship system is an absolute workout. You don't want to piss anyone off. You need to know who's allied with whom, who hates whom, and what's socially acceptable, while all of this information is constantly shifting. You have to soak up a lot of relational data, and then know when to deploy that knowledge at the right time. The more people in your social group, the harder it all becomes. I get exhausted just reading this, so imagine the amount of energy your brain uses every day. That's why we have big, fancy ones.

This relationship focus is also why we're really good at learning. Humans don't have to wait for new genes to drop in order to get a new trait or skill. We can just watch Bill next door, and do whatever he does. The influence of our family, neighbors, and yes, even influencers, is how we learn. We have a word for this—"culture." And it's the newest and fastest form of evolution there is.

If you're waiting for the downside, here it is. Sometimes we influence one another a little too much. In Bowen theory, there is a phrase for how we let people's reactions, real or imaginary, affect us—it's called being relationship-oriented. Some humans are more relationship-oriented than others. They invest a great deal of energy in trying to be what others want them to be. Or in making others what they want them to be. We owe this variation to our families, our genes, and other environmental factors. For example, a family that's experienced a great deal of generational trauma is probably going to be more nervous about upsetting someone. You can't blame them for that.

How relationship-oriented is your thinking? Take a look at this list.

CONSIDER HOW MUCH TIME YOU SPEND:

- Wondering what someone thinks about you.
- Assuming you are annoying people.

- Detecting potential disapproval or distress in others.
- Trying to be the kind of person others want you to be.
- Trying to get others to behave better or differently.
- Worrying about people's potential reactions to your choices.
- Trying to gain approval, agreement, and attention from others.

I don't know about you, but I look at these examples and think, *Woof.* It's humbling to think about how much energy we spend focusing on others. Being relationship-oriented is not the same thing as *valuing* your relationships. It's about trying to control an uncontrollable variable—other people. In his work with families, Murray Bowen observed how a person who invests their energy in trying to manage others (or letting others manage them) has little energy left to think for themselves or pursue their own direction in life. They give up what he called self. "Self" is just a catchall term for being able to think, and then act based on that thinking. Another great thing that humans can do. To have a choice in what you do, rather than living life as a series of automatic emotional reactions. Sounds nice, right?

STOP "FIXING" AND ZOOM OUT

Humans love to fix. It's in our DNA, like a shark who has to swim. We can't help it that our brains are brilliantly fashioned to pursue solutions to problems. But sometimes we chase after things that aren't all that important to us. Like a graduate degree, a thinner body, a million Instagram followers, or, like my twelve-year-old self, a closet full of Beanie Babies. This pursuit manifests in therapy as well. People are driven to borrow answers, to fix, before they're clear about what they think is the best way forward. Because when you're upset, any direction is better than the discomfort it takes to stand still and know your own mind.

Keen on keeping the group calm, we can become obsessed with solving relationship problems. People often come to therapy very intent on fixing a relationship before they have done much thinking about it. Marie spent a lot of time describing the fights between her and Jake. She exhausted a great deal of energy reading Jake's moods, trying not to upset him, or trying to teach him how to not upset her. "I need Jake to not get so anxious when I'm annoyed with him," she'd say, over and over. If you had asked Jake what he needed, he probably would have said, "I need Marie not to get so annoyed with me when I'm busy."

You can see the dilemma here. When our fate depends on other people changing, we get stuck. Jake and Marie were so finely tuned to fluctuations in each other's moods that they couldn't tolerate each other's distress. They craved closeness, but also found it unbearable. They were investing (and wasting) a lot of energy trying to fashion each other into a calmer, more thoughtful partner. And if anyone's ever tried to make you a better partner, you know how allergic we are to these efforts. When two people are trying to change each other, with neither giving in, Bowen theory calls this "conflict." Conflict doesn't have to involve screaming; it's often much subtler. And it's one of the patterns a relationship system uses to manage anxiety.

Most people understand, at least intellectually, that the solution to anxious fixing isn't more of it. But that's exactly what many people do. In therapy, Marie wanted to use a magnifying glass (or sometimes an electron microscope) on her relationship. But there was more to her story than the conflict with Jake. Marie brought less self to other arenas in her life. She was frozen on the career ladder, uncertain if she should keep climbing or jump off. She felt overwhelmed by the expectations of family members she rarely saw. By focusing on one symptom—her relationship conflict—she forgot that there were multiple avenues for working on maturity.

One thing that helped was the decision to zoom out—way, way out—and see the bigger story. The story of Marie's own family across the generations, and how they handled the delicate balance of individuality and togetherness in relationships—the true challenge of being human.

Marie talked about her family and the problems they had faced over the generations. And I tried to ask questions that helped both of us get a sense of how relationship-oriented the people in her family were:

- How much were people permitted to be themselves?
- Who had to hide their beliefs or parts of their identity to keep things calm?
- Whom did other people try to fix or label as the problem?
- Who moved away or disappeared when things became intense?
- What were parents' reactions to their children's choices?

Questions engage our best thinking in a way that answers cannot. They also steer us away from self-criticism when we begin to see our emotional inheritance, the patterns we learn from our family.

Marie could look at her family history and see the origins of her sensitivity to others. A grandfather who felt intense pressure to follow the family business and died young from a heart attack. A grandmother who immigrated and resented her children's assimilation to the new culture. Marie saw a history of marriages where one partner eclipsed the other, making all the choices and directing their beliefs. There were parents with substance use problems and children (like herself) who learned how to be careful not to upset them. A history of people acting and reacting to one another, in the best way they knew how.

We look for the patterns not to blame our ancestors, but to take the bull's-eye off a single person's back. There is no one person who needs to be "fixed." And there is no one relationship that has to be the focus of therapy. Every human interaction is an opportunity for learning to build a self. And every movement toward maturity benefits our relationships. When we limit our scope to the current fire, we usually end up getting burned.

THREE REACTIONS THAT STEAL OUR ENERGY

We like to think that humans are complex, unknowable unicorns. But much of the time, our behaviors are predictable reactions driven by anxiety. Bowen theory uses a very simple definition of "anxiety," which is also sometimes called "emotional reactivity." It's simply a response to a real or an imagined threat. Bowen saw the family as an emotional unit, or emotional organism, that is trying its best to manage anxiety. This is also true for any group where people are significant to one another. If you only look at an individual, you miss seeing how others participate in, and reinforce, the patterns that are activated to manage the threat. You see the predictable ways we respond to pressure from others. These patterns will be defined and discussed at length in the book, but here's a simple way to start thinking about them.

THE MORE SENSITIVE WE ARE TO PEOPLE'S REACTIONS, THE MORE WE:

- Accommodate, trying to be what others want us to be.
- Act out, rebelling or attacking the other.
- Avoid, distancing from others or cutting off the relationship.

I call these the Neapolitan ice cream of reactions. They are safe, familiar options when anxiety is high. Strawberry, vanilla, and chocolate are fine, but there's not usually much self in them. They are automatic and emotionally driven. They are not responses based on reasoning, or one's own beliefs or principles. And when we limit ourselves to these options, we miss out on the other flavors. Because there are other ways of relating to people than giving in, fighting back, or getting the hell out of town.

Accommodating	Acting out	Avoiding
Agreeing with people to keep things calm.	Playing devil's advocate to upset people.	Sticking to superficial conversation topics.
Hiding your beliefs to not upset others.	Acting less capable than you really are.	Automatically cutting off from anxious relationships.
Giving in to others' demands.	Attacking back when provoked.	Only making duty visits to see family.
Being over-responsible for others.	Rejecting beliefs without using your own thinking.	Never having in-person conversations.
Letting others be over-responsible for you.	Regressing to your younger self.	Not sharing beliefs that are important to you.

Marie could see these patterns at work in her relationship with Jake. She was quick to give in and attend events that didn't interest her. And when she got tired of accommodating, she would act out by picking fights or giving him the cold shoulder. But these patterns existed in her other relationships as well. Marie tried to live up to her mother's career expectations (accommodating). When she did call her parents, she played it safe, only talking about superficial things (avoiding). On the rare visits home, Marie quickly regressed to her teenage self, slamming doors or starting arguments at dinner (acting out). Though not ideal, these reactions felt safer than simply being herself. Sharing her interests, joys, challenges, and beliefs with her family felt way too risky.

HOW YOU FIND YOURSELF

Marie and Jake persisted in their intense focus on each other. Their conflict escalated when Jake begged her to attend yet another social event for his school. Unwilling to put up with the blowback from saying no, she tagged along, nursing a Diet Coke while Jake extroverted himself around the room. After tracking his movements with great resentment, Marie bolted without a goodbye. Jake came home at 3 A.M., drunk and grumpy, and Marie, still fuming, pretended to be asleep.

Some people might call this relationship "codependent." I'm not a fan of the term. People tend to use it like a diagnosis—something a relationship either is or isn't. Bowen proposed that someone is always losing at least a little bit of self in a relationship. It's impossible to interact with anyone and not adjust yourself a smidge, or vice versa. The question is, to what degree? Holding on to yourself is a universal, human challenge, sometimes an easier one than others. So don't be hard on yourself when you feign interest yet again in March Madness or the Marvel Cinematic Universe. Just be curious about how to lead with more of your own thinking.

A decision with less self is automatic and rooted in emotion. One with more self has that heartbeat or two's worth of time when you can ask yourself, *What is my responsibility here?* It sounds so simple, but in the heat of conflict, it can feel impossible. We are swept along by the tide of emotion, grasping for familiar patterns rather than steering our own ship.

Think about the directions you've pursued in your life. How did you arrive at these decisions? We are often so focused on the content of our decisions (what we accomplished, where we failed, etc.) that we forget to look at the decision-making process. How much self, or how little, was at work in your choices?

MORE SELF

- Ability to override automatic, emotional reactions.
- Decisions based on thinking/principles.
- Less need for others to be like you.
- Greater ability to evaluate yourself.

LESS SELF

- Driven by automatic, emotional responses.
- More thinking borrowed from others.
- Focus on managing others.
- Focus on others' real or imagined reactions.

Marie began to see that her efforts to keep Jake happy (and to change him) had been automatic, emotionally driven, and largely ineffective. They mirrored the pattern in her family, where one partner was eclipsed by the other. Marie needed a strategy that had more self in it. She had to think about how she wanted to conduct herself, and how she wanted to respond when Jake was distressed or pressuring her. Here's what it can look like in the brain when you're making this shift toward building self.

LESS SELF: My boyfriend expects too much of me.
MORE SELF: I need to get clearer with myself (and him) about what I can and cannot do.

LESS SELF: I need my partner not to panic when I'm feeling annoyed with them.
MORE SELF: How can I focus on managing my own distress?

LESS SELF: If I sigh dramatically enough, perhaps he will ask what's wrong with me.
MORE SELF: What do I think is important to communicate?

LESS SELF: I wonder if the next fight will destroy our relationship.
MORE SELF: What might happen if I focused on changing my part in relationship patterns?

Marie also knew that she had even more work to do outside the relationship. It would take energy to build friendships outside of Jake's grad school friends. More research to learn about jobs outside her career path. More effort to pursue relationships with her parents than to maintain a superficial distance. But this is the shift from borrowing to building a self.

Moving away from a relationship-oriented life isn't a fast process. But it's a lot easier to interrupt your automatic reactions if you've given yourself an alternative path. Marie had invested so much energy into trying to make her boyfriend less of an extrovert, and in trying to make herself more of one. Now she had a new directive for herself—

dialing down her anxiety enough so that she could really observe the relationship. If they were allowing each other to be themselves, would they be compatible as a couple? Whether they stayed together or broke up, Marie wanted the decision to come from her best thinking. From real observations, rather than the anxious "what-ifs" that crept into her brain at night.

Marie also tried to pepper her days with more self-direction. She made attempts to reconnect with old friends in the area. She began to share more about her life with her parents, even if they disapproved or sounded uninterested. She turned down more of Jake's invitations and ended her softball career. And she stopped trying to teach him not to grumble when she passed on a social event. Instead, she expressed her interest in spending time with him one-on-one, whether it was taking a walk in the evening or hitting up the bookstore together. They both tried to take a few minutes each morning to set down their phones and talk about their day. Over time, she found that these connecting points helped reduce the anxiety when they spent time apart.

By no means was this a perfect process. The urge to focus on Jake's mood, to see more love and attention as the only remedy for their intensity, was always hovering in the background. And there certainly were moments when Jake tried to make Marie more like himself, just as there were moments when Marie attempted to squash his earnest dedication to networking or group sports. But they were moving in the right direction. Marie was getting a glimpse of what it was like to operate more as a self. To stay thoughtful when Jake was reactive, instead of matching him pout for pout. To stay curious when she was lonely, eager to find joy in new friendships. To define her thinking to Jake, rather than waiting for him to make his best guess.

Reducing relationship orientation isn't about giving up on a relationship. Nor is it about putting up with bad behavior. By adding more self to the equation, we give the relationship a chance to succeed (or not) based on reality. Not our worst fears or greatest fantasies of what other people could be. And we allow ourselves to make choices based on our best thinking, rather than the anxiety of the moment. Slowly, Marie was taking the pressure off her relationship to regulate her mood or direct her steps. By relieving this pressure, we give our relationships a chance to be what they were meant to be. A place where we can be ourselves, and permit others to do the same.

NOW IT'S TIME to put your thinking into action. Set aside some time to work through each exercise. Consider keeping a journal with your answers, so you can revisit your insights and apply them to your daily life. Or generate your own homework that best fits your challenges.

EXERCISE 1: **Being what others want you to be.** Be honest with yourself. What percentage of your daily energy is caught up in trying to be what others want you to be? Are you answering emails at 10 P.M.? Furiously cleaning the house before a friend pops over? Spending way too much time finding the perfect filter for a photo? Make a list of some recent activities that were more about trying to manage other people's reactions than about living out your best thinking.

EXERCISE 2: **How much self is in your relationships?** Make a list of the ten most important relationships in your life. What are the relationships where you feel like you bring the most "self"? Where you're able to talk about your joys, challenges, and interests with less worry about how the other will respond? What are the relationships where you tend to be more relationship-oriented? Where are you more willing to let others change you, or more interested in trying to change them? Now rank them one to ten from the "least self" to "most self." Look at the names near the bottom of the list and think about how you can lead with more authenticity and thoughtfulness in those relationships—and how you can let others do the same.

EXERCISE 3: **Learn something about your family**. It can be helpful to learn about how relationship pressures played a role in your family's history. When you look at your past generations, can you tell who anxiously adjusted to keep things calm? Who tended to decide what others should be or do? Who disappeared, or cut off, because they couldn't stand the pressures? Write down any thoughts you have about how people pressured others to change, or how they changed to please others. I hope that these patterns can help you think about your current relationships a little differently. If you're missing information, think about the people you can contact to learn more about the family.

CHAPTER NUGGETS

- Many of our choices in life are borrowed from other people. This is because we are social animals. We care about how people react, or might react.
- How much we let other people's reactions influence us is how relationship-oriented we are. A person who is more relationship-oriented has less energy to pursue their own goals and interests.
- Self is the ability to act based on your own thinking and to choose how you respond to others. A person with less self is driven largely by automatic, emotional reactions.
- Learning to be less relationship-oriented requires you to give up trying to fix others in your life.
- One relationship pattern for managing anxiety is

conflict. Conflict occurs when two people are trying to change each other, and neither gives in.

- Looking at the multigenerational history of a family (or group/organization) helps you broaden the focus by zooming out and seeing the larger patterns.
- Anxiety is a response to a real or imagined threat. The family is an emotional unit that is trying its best to manage anxiety through predictable patterns.
- Three ways we respond to relationship pressure include accommodating, acting out, and avoiding. These reactions can be limiting, not reflecting the way we'd like to represent ourselves in relationships.
- Rather than focusing on others, consider who you want to be in important relationships. What's worth pursuing, and what's worth sharing with others?

2

THE COST OF KEEPING PEOPLE HAPPY

"Do I wanna call my dad? No, I don't wanna call my dad. Do you wanna call your dad?"

—Kendall Roy, *Succession*

ALEX'S PARENTS HAD always called her their greatest accomplishment. The only child of two beloved high school marching band directors, she described herself as a high achiever who'd always enjoyed praise and attention from her parents, her teachers, or the pack of teenagers who helped raise her. What Alex didn't realize, however, was how devotion to their daughter had stabilized her parents' marriage. It kept them a tight-knit, happy trio, until her father went and blew it all up.

When Alex left for college, the creeping distance in her parents' marriage became a chasm. Her father, Dan, ended up having an affair with his high school girlfriend, also known as the flute player who got away. When Alex's mother found out, the family, and the band's chance for a state championship, promptly imploded. Fast-forward a few years, and Alex, twenty-five years old, had a stepmother and three teenage stepsiblings. Not to mention a mother who wanted a lot of her attention, and a father who now felt like a stranger.

Dan begged Alex to do family therapy with him. He hated the distance he felt with his daughter, who seemed uninterested in getting to know her stepmom and stepsiblings. Alex had been unwilling to part from her now single mom over the holidays, and her sporadic conversations with her father always felt cold and superficial. Dan spoke of their closeness when she was younger—how they were joined at the hip when they played music together or dissected the drama of episodes of *Vampire Diaries*. Now he felt that he was losing her. "How long is she going to punish me for this affair?" he wondered out loud.

From Alex's perspective, Dan didn't seem to have much time for her. Now directing the band in a neighboring town, he was always busy with rehearsals or chauffeuring his stepchildren. His invites came at odd times or the last minute. Could she talk at midnight on Tuesday? Could she drive to his school during the workday to grab lunch? He'd invite her on vacations with his new family, but only a week before their departure date. When he wasn't distant, Dan communicated via long, rambling texts about the state of their relationship and how sad it made him. How he would do anything to make things better. Alex was quick to point out the discrepancy between his words and actions.

During our meetings, Alex was mostly quiet. Dan was very focused on how Alex was feeling. He'd interrupt me to check in on her. If she became emotional, he'd lose his train of thought. They were so finely tuned to each other's reactions, there was little self-direction in all the reactivity.

Could one of them put their head above water and begin to think differently about the dilemma?

HOW STUCK TOGETHER ARE YOU?

People often think that the solution to relationship conflict is more focus on the relationship—giving more love and attention to each other. But an intense focus is part of the problem. We don't thrive or think well when other people are anxiously monitoring us.

Despite the distance in their relationship, Dan and Alex were stuck in relationship orientation. They both devoted an enormous amount of time to thinking about the other, imagining what they were doing, or how they might react to their messages (or lack thereof). Though they felt far apart, they were stuck together. Bowen used the term "fusion" to describe the level of stuck-togetherness in a relationship or relationship system. When there's more fusion, people are more likely to make decisions that keep the relationship stable or harmonious, even at the cost of their own best thinking.

Our stuck-togetherness as humans is both a feature and a bug. It's part of our evolutionary heritage. Genes that promoted altruism and cooperation won out in the natural selection process, so our big brains are built for reading the room, for taking the temperature in our relationships. The ability to guess what another person is thinking and feeling is essential for group cooperation. Psychologists sometimes call it the "nine-month revolution," when an infant begins to read the cues of an adult to evaluate their environment. It's sort of like looking at the flight attendant's face when the plane is tossing in heavy turbulence. They're likely to know something we don't.

In anxious times, these evolutionary superpowers can get stuck in high gear. The fusion in Alex and Dan's relationship made it hard to separate one person's emotions from the other's. Dan couldn't tolerate Alex's discomfort with his new life. So he would stall his invitations, or cancel on her at the last minute. Or he would spend half a therapy session checking on how she was doing. When fusion is high, relationships often shift between an intense closeness and an allergic distance.

FUSION CAN LOOK LIKE:

- Needing a lot of emotional support.
- Being highly sensitive to others' anxiety.
- Quickly adopting (or rejecting) others' beliefs.
- Wanting to create a good impression.
- Feeling pressured by others' opinions.
- Feeling allergic to others' opinions.
- Succeeding when you get praise.
- Flailing when you don't get praise.
- Struggling to let others be themselves.

So much of our functioning is propped up by positive reactions from others. Many people are very high achieving at work, only to be brought low by a slight criticism or passive aggressive text. In family therapy, I've watched an eye roll or quivering lip from a family member make another person's mind go blank. The invisible attachment to others is always there to some degree, promoting or derailing our functioning.

THE RISE OF THE ACCOMMODATOR

When a relationship is high in fusion, people may be quick to accommodate the other. You might spend a great deal of energy trying to be what others want you to be. Maybe you dress nice because you don't want to embarrass your spouse. Or speak up in class because your professor looks nervous. Or pretend to agree when your best friend is on a political rant. Accommodation creates calmness at a cost. At some point, the bill comes due.

WHAT WE LOSE WHEN WE ACCOMMODATE:

- The chance to teach our brain how to tolerate disagreement.
- The opportunity to define our beliefs to others.
- The practice of letting others be responsible for themselves.
- The joy of talking about what's interesting to us.
- The boundaries that help us function as individuals.
- The joy of watching our kids become independent.
- The free time to pursue what's important to us.
- The ability to self-regulate when others are anxious.

We tend to think of people pleasers as human doormats. But accommodating is often subtler than we realize. Interaction by interaction, we make minor adjustments based on our audience and their mood. It's the way you tell a story to a close friend, then tell a slightly tamer version to your grandma. The way you let your teenager leave a mess because you can't handle another battle of wills. Accommodating is a necessary part of life, but left unchecked, it can become our autopilot.

At first glance, Dan and Alex might seem unaccommodating to each other. Both argued that the other was inconsiderate. But look closely, and you'll see the anxious attempts to calm down the other. Alex was in therapy to appease her dad. Dan had stopped asking Alex to visit his new family because he knew it upset her. Alex was willing to meet her dad at the last minute, even when it was inconvenient. Excessive accommodating was part of the problem. They were so focused on each other that they'd given up a lot of self in the process. Neither had any operating instructions about who they wanted to be in this relationship.

In their attempts to appease the other, Dan and Alex paid a great price. Dan lost the chance to enjoy watching Alex build relationships with his wife and stepchildren. Alex lost free time and energy when she worried about her dad's long, angsty texts. They were both losing the chance at a relationship that didn't feel like a five-alarm fire every time they communicated. They wanted their relationship to be freer and easier, but how?

A FERRIS WHEEL OF FUSION

To begin to resolve fusion in a relationship, you must consider how you use the relationship to manage anxiety. Every relationship system, including your family, uses predictable patterns to stay stable, patterns Bowen called the "emotional process." If you want to change your part in a relationship, you have to focus on the process, not just the content of your squabbles. Mapping actions and reactions can help us begin to move out of this predictability. To unstick ourselves.

Here's the process that Dan and Alex described to me: Late at night, Dan would begin to feel sad about his relationship with Alex. He would express his anxious distress to her via text. Annoyed by his intense feelings, Alex would

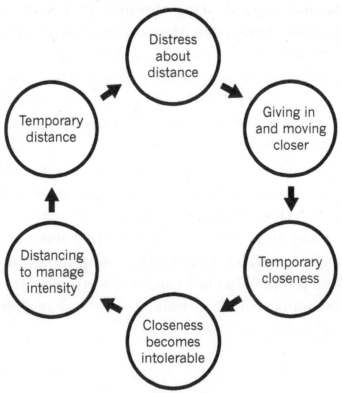

Figure 1. The Ferris wheel of fusion.

accommodate, agreeing to grab a quick lunch or have an awkward dinner with the stepfamily. But Alex usually felt resentful and prickly about the accommodation. Tuned in to her discomfort, Dan tried his best to put her at ease, showering her with love and attention during these meetings. Allergic to this intense focus, Alex would begin to pull away and keep her distance. This distance kept things calm, until Dan would begin to feel upset about their relationship once again. Sure enough, he'd fire off a text that would restart the whole cycle. A sort of Ferris wheel of fusion.

If you look at this cycle, you can see why it's useful to think of accommodating (or people pleasing) as part of a process *rather* than a personality trait. In tense times, we get caught in patterns that are about keeping things calm, rather than relating to one another. We might accommodate, avoid, or act out. We dance back and forth between intense closeness and allergic distance. We react in ways that relieve anxiety as quickly as possible.

How do you get off this Ferris wheel? You begin to think about your part in the cycle. Every point is an opportunity to muster some emotional courage, to not do what you would normally do to calm things down. To disrupt the predictable chain of events and bring some thinking to the game. Either Alex or Dan could change the pattern. When one person functions differently, the ride grinds to a halt. A new path lights up.

THE THIRD WAY

Our relationships can be so much more than anxious people pleasing. It's possible to be in a relationship, but a little outside of the emotional process. And some people manage to do this better than others. Bowen called this variable "differentiation of self"—the ability to stay in contact with others, while thinking and acting for one's self. It is the central concept of Bowen theory and the main idea in this book.

Sometimes I call differentiation the "third way"—a way

to relate to people without giving in to relationship pressure or giving up on the relationship. In relationships high in fusion, working on differentiation of self is very difficult. But that's where it counts the most. If you can be yourself in those relationships, you have a higher chance of representing yourself and your beliefs authentically with anyone.

Bowen envisioned differentiation of self as a continuum, a scale where people range from low to high levels of self. Where do you get your level of differentiation? It has a lot to do with how your family operates. Some families are more emotionally interdependent than others, meaning they rely more on relationship patterns to manage stress. Growing up, some people have more freedom to develop a self, while others have less. Some kids get the anxious focus, and they're pulled more often into the patterns the system uses to manage stress, while other siblings may escape this involvement to a larger degree.

A higher level of differentiation doesn't imply a rugged individualism (often lauded in Western cultures) any more than a lower level would imply a reliance on others. Differentiation reflects a more flexible capacity for connection and self-direction, a mature dependence on others while also being responsible for oneself. It is less about how we relate to others, and more about the *intensity* of the relating. For example, a highly differentiated person might choose to end a relationship because they're acting according to their own beliefs. A less differentiated person might cut off a relationship as a way of quickly managing anxiety. You have the same choice being made, but each person may be operating with different levels of self. Less self isn't "bad." It's just less flexible, with more reliance on those patterns we see in any relationship system. Strawberry, vanilla, chocolate.

Bowen saw two variables impacting the capacity of an emotional system (e.g. your family, your work team, your congregation) to meet challenges: the level of anxiety, and the level of differentiation. While we cannot always control the level of anxiety in the system, we can do something about our level of differentiation. But working on differentiation isn't a worksheet, or a five-step technique, or a three-week course. It is the long-term effort toward finding some self in how you relate to significant people in your life. The work of striving to see patterns and stepping outside of them at least a little bit.

Alex and Dan began to think about new ways of relating to each other, outside of the predictable patterns that often ensnared them. What responses weren't about responding to pressure? Responses that didn't look like giving in (accommodating) or giving up (avoiding) on the relationship? Here are a few situations they thought about.

SITUATION 1: My dad sends me long, rambling texts about his distress.

ACCOMMODATING: I send a long reply, reassuring him that I love him.

AVOIDING: I ignore it.

THIRD WAY: I could call him tomorrow and tell him when it is convenient to see him.

SITUATION 2: My daughter seems uncomfortable when she comes over for dinner.

ACCOMMODATING: I mediate the conversations between her and others.

AVOIDING: I stop inviting her to dinner and just see her one-on-one.

THIRD WAY: I give her space to adjust to this new environment. I focus on calming myself down instead.

SITUATION 3: I can feel my daughter distancing from me.
ACCOMMODATING: I apologize for being a terrible dad. I tell her I'll do anything to make it better.
AVOIDING: I don't initiate contact and wait for her to contact me first.
THIRD WAY: I let her know when I'd like to spend time with her and catch up. I manage my own distress about the distance without overinvolving her.

Differentiation looks different for each individual. It's less about what you're doing, and more about the amount of brainpower behind it. Have you thought about the best response to a challenging situation? Or are you just trying to calm things down as quickly as possible? There's a difference between giving someone space and anxiously distancing. Just as there is between thoughtful agreement and anxious people pleasing. It takes practice to look underneath the surface of our choices and see the emotional process at work. But it can make all the difference.

YOUR FIRST DAY OF SCHOOL

Every parent remembers their child's first day of school. The day before my daughter started preschool, her principal sent out an email encouraging adults to make a fast and calm drop-off on day one. "Your energy during drop-off, your thoughts, body language, and level of confidence," she wrote, "set the tone for how the child feels about being dropped off."

Well, damn, I thought. *Doesn't that just sum it up.*

No adult would argue that an anxious, clingy drop-off is what's best for their kid. We understand that our own self-regulation is a gift to children. Yet we often do the exact opposite in adult relationships. People act as though a rambling text at 3 A.M. is going to patch things up with a boyfriend, or that venting to a colleague is going to improve their relationship with the boss. When a friend is in a bad mood, maybe you've tried to anxiously fix their problem rather than staying calm and asking good questions. Managing ourselves is often our last thought when we sense distress in others.

Dan and Alex needed their own first day of school. And since they were both grown-ups, either of them could set a new tone in the relationship. Dan could give Alex space to figure out how she wanted to relate to his new wife. He could stop and calm himself down before blasting off an anxious message to her. Or Alex could say, "Not now," when her dad tried to make plans at the last minute. She could ask about holiday plans, instead of waiting for an invitation. And they could both stop evaluating the relationship based on how the other person felt!

If one of them could make any of these moves, school would officially be in session. It would be a time for learning how to stand like a self, rather than rolling around in the fusion.

A LESS DIFFERENTIATED PERSON:

- Ignores the role their own emotional reactivity plays in relationships.

- Works on appeasing others instead of managing themselves.
- Treats people like they are incapable.
- Treats relationship challenges like they are impending catastrophes.

A MORE DIFFERENTIATED PERSON:

- Observes their own reactivity and its influence.
- Works on managing self rather than managing others.
- Treats people like they are capable.
- Can take on relationship challenges with more curiosity.

When fusion is high in a relationship, that second list does not come naturally to us. After all, humans evolved to preserve relationship harmony with great efficiency. Focusing on others is not a type of dysfunction—it's a behavioral adaptation that keeps things calm to a degree. Don't be so hard on yourself if you slip back to your factory settings.

Interrupting people pleasing can feel like a fake-it-till-you-make-it approach. But it has less to do with willpower, and more with how we think about the problem. Bowen described the power of observing our relationships like you would a football game from the top of the stadium. If you can see the patterns, the emotional process beneath the content of our complaints, you will begin to think differently about relationship challenges. It becomes harder to label villains and heroes. You might focus less on whether people like you or not. You'll see the paradox of being human, the reality that we crave closeness as much as we're itching to get away from it. From the top of the stadium, you realize that the only variable you can tinker with is yourself.

BECOMING A SYSTEMS THINKER

When Alex and Dan stood on top of the stadium, their story felt less like a tragedy. It became a more predictable story, one where family members struggled to function as individuals after a stressful divorce. Over time, it became a tale of two grown-ups, each of whom had a chance to work on differentiation.

When you can take a story of back-and-forth blaming and turn it into a map of the emotional process, you become a systems thinker. Bowen described this as developing emotional objectivity, the capacity to see how the relationship system works rather than relying on simple cause-and-effect explanations (e.g. "I'm this way *because* my mother did *X*"). While the stories we tell have some truth to them, they ultimately keep us stuck in relationship orientation. Thinking about your own part in the patterns, as well as the multigenerational history of these patterns, can help you feel less stuck. Here's what shifting from storytelling to systems thinking looked like for Alex and Dan.

STORYTELLING: My dad has no sense of boundaries.
SYSTEMS THINKING: How did his family relate to one another in challenging times? How much were people permitted to be themselves?

STORYTELLING: My dad doesn't have time for me anymore.

SYSTEMS THINKING: Distancing is one way he's dealt with the anxiety in the system.

STORYTELLING: My daughter is punishing me for having an affair.
SYSTEMS THINKING: Distancing is one way she's dealt with anxiety in the system.

STORYTELLING: We're not as close as we used to be.
SYSTEMS THINKING: The pressure to be close can make us more sensitive to each other. What we label "closeness" may be a lack of self in how we relate to each other.

By using systems thinking, Dan and Alex could see that anxious closeness wasn't real closeness. And anxious distance wasn't true breathing space. By operating more as individuals, they could have a more authentic and rewarding relationship. One of them could disagree, or say no, without feeling like estrangement was on the horizon. Like many relationship challenges, the stakes were much lower than they appeared.

Often in families, one person is more interested in interrupting patterns than others. But that's all it takes. When one individual is operating with more flexibility, with more thoughtfulness, the whole system is a little less reliant on the patterns it uses to keep things calm. In this case, Alex was more curious about shaking things up. Dan was too worried about her, too focused on how she was feeling when we met. But Alex was paying attention, and she tried to keep the focus on herself. She hoped that managing her own anxiety more responsibly would improve her relationship with her dad. And she got better at not hopping back on the Ferris wheel.

Alex recognized the importance of pursuing relationships with her stepmom and stepsiblings. Diving in, despite the awkwardness, was more desirable than a lifetime of dancing anxiously around them. When she started moving toward them for her own benefit, not as an attempt to please her dad, she found that there were things she loved about being a stepsister. But Alex also got more comfortable doing what worked best with her schedule. She reached out to her dad to schedule one-on-one time, and when he sent an invite that wasn't convenient for her, she told him so.

At first, Alex tried teaching her dad how to not send her long, emotional text messages at all hours. If you've ever tried to teach a family member how to manage their anxiety differently, you can imagine how well this went. Realizing this wasn't a move toward differentiation, Alex changed course and communicated to Dan (via phone call) how she was going to respond to texts in the future. "I'm not going to talk about feelings via text," she told him, setting a clear boundary. "I'm willing to listen to your thoughts when we talk on the phone or meet in person." Notice the I's in those statements. They communicate, "Here's what you can expect from me. This is where I stand." This is differentiation of self. It requires no cooperation, no particular response from another person.

When Dan observed Alex making moves toward differentiation, his anxiety increased. He accused Alex of being insensitive and cold. He commented that he didn't know who she was anymore. Over time, however, he couldn't deny that their relationship had calmed down. He saw how Alex was working on relating to her stepfamily. He knew she was earnest in her efforts to spend time with him, even if she didn't respond to every text he sent. While he was mourning the loss of the fusion in the relationship, his daughter was becoming more of a self. Their relationship was changing, but for the better. Dan realized his fears of estrangement weren't rooted in reality.

This family story fascinates me because it holds a valuable truth—sometimes the younger generation gets to represent the mind-set of the drop-off parent. Because there's no monopoly on maturity when we're all adults. Your relationship with a parent is perhaps *the* hardest place to bust out of emotional patterns. Not everyone is as lucky as Alex, having a parent who is slow to learn but willing to stay in contact when we set boundaries with them. But if you see an opening, a way of operating differently in these important relationships, consider that it's never too late to set a new tone. To manage yourself a little more responsibly. Don't underestimate what working on differentiation in family relationships can teach you.

And the next time you catch yourself in people-pleasing mode? Just pay attention to the process. Stand on top of the stadium for a bit, and then try making a move that's born out of good thinking, not an attempt to make people feel happy or behave better. Your only job is to be your most responsible self, a job that will keep you busy for the rest of your life. A person who is working on differentiation of self is giving their relationships a chance to be something different. The less focused we are on keeping others happy, the more we can be truly present in the lives of those we love.

EXERCISE 1: **How do you accommodate?** Make a quick list of all the ways you make small or large adjustments to keep people calm or happy. Do you edit out those extra exclamation points in an email so you don't alarm anyone with your enthusiasm? Do you answer the phone at all hours because your mother expects it? Accommodating isn't good or bad. Just pay attention to the pattern and ask yourself, *Is this who I want to be?*

EXERCISE 2: **What's your Ferris wheel?** When you feel frustrated with someone, take a breath and see how much you can map out the pattern of actions and reactions in the relationship. How do each of you deal with the tension? Do you give in and accommodate, or give up and avoid? Where are there opportunities to try a third way, to work on differentiation of self?

EXERCISE 3: **Get your butt to school.** Most of the time, we're rushing through our day, not paying attention to our emotions and how we manage them. What would it look like to have a "first day of school" with your kids, a coworker, or an anxious friend? What would it look like to manage yourself more responsibly? Write down your ideas.

CHAPTER NUGGETS

- Another word for relationship orientation is "fusion." When fusion is high in a relationship, it's difficult to separate your thoughts and emotions from the other person's. Decisions are made based on the reactions or potential reactions of the other person.

- People can get stuck in a people-pleasing mode as a response to fusion. This constant accommodating is one way we give up self to keep a relationship calm.

- The emotional process consists of the common, predictable patterns that we use to manage anxiety in relationships.

- Differentiation of self is the degree to which a person can think and act for one's self while in relationship with others.

- Working on differentiation often requires a willingness not to do what you might normally do to manage anxiety. It is a way of being less pulled by the emotional process.

- Seeing relationship patterns can help us shift out of blaming and practice being a systems thinker. A systems thinker can see one's part in the emotional process, and begin to respond more thoughtfully to relationship challenges.

3

HOW WE END UP
BORROWING OUR BELIEFS

"I just think I want someone to tell me how to live my life, Father, because so far I think I've been getting it wrong, and I know that's why people want people like you in their lives, because you just tell them how to do it."

—Fleabag, *Fleabag*

AT SEVENTY-THREE, MARGARET was still getting to know herself. She was a retired high school biology teacher, mother of two, and grandmother of seven. And she'd just taken a great leap in life, moving with her husband into a retirement community. The attractive campus of Friendship Village was a lot like high school, full of cliques, queen bees, and unspoken rules, as well as a killer baked potato bar. Facing the social pressures of a new environment, Margaret let me in on a secret: she didn't feel like she'd lived a life of strong belief. Most of her decisions had been attempts to keep people happy. And she worried she'd fallen into this pattern yet again.

Like any human's, Margaret's life was a combination of courageous decisions and anxious accommodations to others. She was the middle child of working-class Southern Baptists who'd scrimped to send her to college. Her junior year, she went and did the unthinkable—married a young professor who was Catholic. Her mother responded by dying a month after they'd eloped. Margaret didn't think she'd singlehandedly killed her mother by picking up a rosary. But it scared her enough that she changed her major from psychology to education, her mother's wish.

Fast-forward fifty years, and Margaret, a student of Bowen theory, saw new opportunities for working on differentiation of self. One year into the COVID-19 pandemic, Margaret felt stuck in relationship orientation. She was too involved in the divorce of her younger son, Grant. She was too quick to follow the advice of her older son, Paul, a doctor who wanted his parents to live like the bubble boy. Meanwhile, the newly vaccinated residents of Friendship Village were partying like it was Woodstock. At Margaret's church, the congregation was torn between getting back to normal and playing it safe. Margaret wasn't sure what she thought. Either way, someone was bound to be upset.

OUR DEEP DESIRE TO FIT IN

In the natural world, blending in with the group is a powerful form of self-defense. Look different from your peers, and you'll catch the eye of a hungry predator. Show up to middle school in the wrong shoes, and you're basically a lone wildebeest on the savannah. Humans are master conformers, and our brains were built to adopt the norms of the family, the peer group, or society. American culture, however, often portrays the human experience as a battle between uniqueness and conformity. Between finding our calling or keeping up with the Joneses. But what if these forces are equally important? What if you being yourself is actually what the group wants? And what if conforming to the group is a useful way to be yourself? The interaction between the individual and the group is much more complex than a tug-of-war.

Humans have a strong drive to direct ourselves, but we also have a strong drive to connect with others. And these drives are in constant tension. Murray Bowen called the forces "individuality" and "togetherness," and he saw them as central to life.

Individuality is the drive to determine one's own thoughts, beliefs, and behaviors.

Togetherness is the drive to think and act like others, or to get others to think and act like we do.

As a high school teacher, Margaret had a front-row seat to this tension. Teenagers want to be unique, but they also desperately want to fit in. Their brains can't really distinguish between what they think of themselves and what other people think of them. And adults aren't much better. Margaret's parents had wanted to raise self-determined kids, so long as this independence led them to a particular church on Sunday and to similar conclusions about the world. Margaret wanted her son to navigate his own divorce, but she couldn't help but swoop in whenever he made questionable choices. Her own church tried to promote good debate in Sunday school, but God forbid you question the upcoming trip to the March for Life. Everywhere we look, the world is telling us, "Be yourself! No, not that way!"

At Friendship Village, Margaret moved around like an anthropologist. She studied how people dressed, what they talked about, and what they didn't talk about. Her brain quietly mapped out the third rails so she could avoid them. But did it have to be this way? Wasn't retirement the time when you could finally be yourself?

In times of great anxiety, the togetherness force takes the wheel. Nothing has ever demonstrated this more clearly to me than the COVID-19 pandemic. In the United States, as people struggled to determine what was safe, they often abandoned this thinking the second anyone had a different opinion. In the early days, before we knew much about the virus, therapy clients would tell me how they'd let people into their house, or agreed to eating inside a restaurant when they didn't feel comfortable doing so. People would shake someone's hand when they offered it because letting it hang there felt impossibly rude. Think about that—hurting someone's feelings felt more threatening than potential illness or even death. Is there any better evidence of how social we humans are? The impulse for togetherness is no easy thing to override.

IN A GROUP HIGH IN TOGETHERNESS:

- People's decisions are based on how others will react.
- People are highly sensitive to one another's reactions.
- It's harder for you to define your own beliefs.
- People are less tolerant of disagreement.
- There is an intense focus on being loved and accepted.

- People will focus on keeping things calm.
- People easily become over-responsible for one another.

WHEN A GROUP HAS A GREATER BALANCE OF INDIVIDUALITY AND TOGETHERNESS:

- People treat one another like they're capable.
- People give you space to generate your own thinking.
- People are less sensitive to others' real or imagined reactions.
- People are more flexible and resourceful when solving problems together.
- People are more genuinely interested in others' thoughts.
- People more easily stay open and connected in anxious times.

Margaret saw a lot of togetherness in her nuclear family. Everyone dutifully followed her son's pandemic recommendations, so he started lecturing everyone about their nutritional or sleep habits as well. Every week, Margaret spent hours on the phone giving advice to her youngest, only to throw her hands up when he went in the opposite direction. Margaret also was quick to tell her quirky husband how to dress and how to talk so that he didn't make them the pariahs of Friendship Village. No wonder Margaret had so little energy left to know her own mind. The boundaries between her responsibilities and everyone else's were blurred beyond recognition.

GROUPS ARE SMARTER THAN YOU

There's a reason why it's hard to trust our own thinking—the group is often smarter than we are. Groups help us survive and thrive in ways we never could as individuals, and they also help us learn more efficiently. Our collective intelligence, known as "swarm intelligence," is often closer to the mark than any random individual's. If you ask one hundred people to guess the number of jelly beans in a jar, the average of all the guesses will be surprisingly close to the correct answer.

Group intelligence ranks high in the animal world. A cockroach community will stick with a crappy shelter because they trust the choice of the previous generations. They know that sticking together, rather than roaming for new real estate, is their best chance of survival. In one famous study, researchers trained dominant chimpanzees to choose a carrot for a snack (rather than tastier grapes). When the other chimpanzees observed their higher-ranking peers choosing the carrot, they ended up making the same choice. They conformed to the decision of their dominant peers.

Why would anyone betray their taste buds for a lousy carrot? The hormone oxytocin likely has something to do it. When we feel calm and connected, oxytocin promotes conformity within the group. It makes us more generous and cooperative than we would be in stressful times. Wanting to be like others is the glue that holds us together, so think twice before you make fun of people for following the advice of their parents or influencers on social media. We look to those we love, or the people getting attention, and we instinctively copy them.

"It takes less than 200 milliseconds for your brain to

register that the group has picked a different answer from yours," writes researcher Robert Sapolsky, "and less than 380 milliseconds for a profile of activation that predicts changing your opinion. Our brains are biased to get along by going along in less than a second."

Margaret felt like a chimpanzee stuck with a carrot. She liked the pomp and grandeur of the Catholic church, the compelling stories of the saints. But did she think it was the best manifestation of the call to love her neighbor? Big no. Had counting Weight Watchers points been the best way to treat her body over the decades? Also no. Was the clump of vitamins her son recommended a great way to start the day? Nope. She expressed her concern that she would end up settling for "good enough" when pursuing relationships at Friendship Village. Would she end up nodding along to political ideas she didn't support, or saying yes to lawn bowling when she'd rather watch paint dry?

THE BELIEF BUFFET

Modern humans face a very modern dilemma. We are members of many groups—groups that may have competing beliefs. We must contend with the beliefs of coworkers, classmates, family, friends, and internet riffraff. Our brains are a veritable buffet of beliefs we've borrowed from our many relationship systems. Crack open my skull, and you'll find traces of my mother's mantras, feisty college professors, old Tumblr posts, and many *Seinfeld* episodes.

We can be quick to criticize how others have adopted their beliefs, and slow to examine our own. A Catholic can meet a Latter-day Saint and ask them, "So you think Jesus just dipped over to America on his way to heaven. That's a little *too* convenient, eh?" But then they may ignore the biological challenges of a virgin birth. You might be critical of folks who support trickle-down economics, but think every story on MSNBC was downloaded straight from reality. Now that I've angered everyone, let me propose an experiment— for just a moment, shift your focus away from the *content* of your beliefs. Think about the *process* by which a belief is adopted. This process has more to do with togetherness than we'd care to admit.

Borrowed beliefs comprise what Bowen called our "pseudo-self." The pseudo-self is a collection of beliefs that may shift based on who's in the room. It bends and evolves with pressure from our relationships. Maybe you adopt beliefs to keep people happy, or reject them to piss people off. Maybe you sound more progressive when your liberal friends are in the room. Maybe you swear off diet culture until your favorite actress recommends her favorite cleanse. Perhaps three drinks is fine when you're with work buddies, but when your teetotaling grandma comes over, you pretend you've never had a sip of beer in your life. So much of us is highly negotiable in the moment.

YOUR PSEUDO-SELF MAY CONSIST OF BELIEFS FROM:

- Your family
- "Experts"
- Political parties
- Religious groups
- Your peers
- Your therapist
- Celebrities

- Social media
- A desperate Google search

We borrow the certainty of others because it is stabilizing. A new parent doesn't always have the time to be thoughtful—they just want advice that will help their baby stop screaming. When a therapist tells you that you're improving, it is deeply calming. When a religious leader tells you that you're on the road to righteousness, or a politician tells you you're on the right side of history, that feels great. Pseudo-self is often how we find the next step or the inspiration to keep going. But going where? And at what cost? The higher the level of anxiety, the more quickly we may adopt beliefs, even those that defy reality. This is how people become radicalized or can't find their way out of a cult.

I'm not saying every group, or every solution, is a cult. If we didn't borrow beliefs, society would collapse tomorrow. We don't have time to reason out every piece of information thrown at us. Sometimes we must choose to trust some people in our lives, whether it's our family, the board of an organization, or dare I say even our elected officials to make the call. In other words, the group wisdom will have to do.

But the human experience does not stop at conformity. We are not limited to the wisdom of the group. We all have beliefs that we approach with more thinking and by less persuasion. Beliefs that can sustain pressure from others, and only change when we're presented with new evidence or experiences. Beliefs that might piss off those we love or fly in the face of our faith or societal expectations. Bowen called these beliefs the "solid self."

The pseudo-self and the solid self are not literal parts of

the brain. They are concepts that can help us think about how we arrive at our beliefs and how we change them. Solid self sounds like a nice idea, but has anyone ever had a belief that wasn't influenced by relationship pressure, at least a little bit? I certainly haven't. But I have beliefs with more "self" in them than others. I have thought a lot about the role of a therapist, about the importance of multigenerational relationships, about why the *Lost* finale was actually good (for the love of god, Sharon, they were *not* dead the whole time!). These beliefs are more solid; they hold up more easily under relationship pressure. And I have others that are more chameleon-like. I'm quick to second-guess how I discipline as a parent. I vacillate over the relevance of organized religion in its current forms. I'm quick to chase after societal definitions of success, or borrow goals that other people set for themselves. These beliefs can change at the first sign of disapproval or shift quickly with changing trends.

Margaret considered the substance of her solid self. As a teacher, she'd developed a clear set of beliefs about how teenagers learn and her role in that learning. These beliefs were based on educational research but also over thirty years in the classroom. Over the years, she'd also teased out the tenets of her faith, many of which were not aligned with the Catholic church. She'd learned to be okay with that reality, without bracing herself for purgatory. She didn't even believe in purgatory.

But Margaret also held beliefs she'd adopted without much reasoning. One was the impulse to not rock the boat in social situations—a value she'd borrowed from her parents. Debates were for the classroom, not Waffle Party Fridays at Friendship Village. But now, she wasn't so sure this

relationship pressure

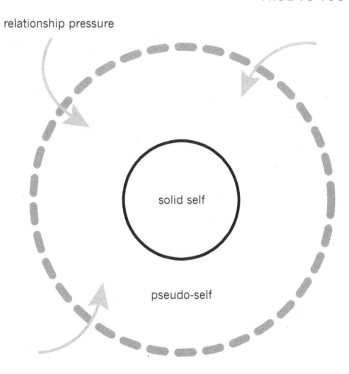

solid self

pseudo-self

Figure 2. Solid and pseudo-self. Note that the pseudo-self has a more penetrable barrier, as it can change with relationship pressure.

was the way to be. Perhaps there was value in being a person who could create some waves.

Margaret also realized she'd been coasting on her son Paul's medical knowledge for years. It made sense to trust a doctor, but she'd watched her responsibility for her own health dip in the face of her son's anxious monitoring. Lately, she hadn't done much thinking about how she wanted to take care of her body or her mind. She'd simply grumbled and followed his instructions.

Margaret also hadn't given much thought to her relationship with her son Grant. Upon closer examination, she realized that she was accommodating, giving him advice and offering constant reassurance to manage his distress. Margaret had conformed to Grant's definition of being a good mother, rather than determining her own. She'd given a lot of thought to what it meant to be a grandmother, but not much about being a parent to adult children. Here was another opportunity for increasing solid self, for working on differentiation.

MIND READERS AND MIND KNOWERS

Around the time you were born, your brain switched on a very important network. It's called the "default mode network," and it runs when we're not focused on any particular motor task. Researchers don't understand everything about this network yet, but they have discovered one of its functions—making sense of our social lives. In these free moments, when we don't appear to be doing anything, our brain is doing deep social calculus. We're reflecting on recent interactions and making predictions about future ones. *Did everyone think I was funny? Did he seem attracted to me?* We're constantly uploading the data we use to guess what a person is thinking, feeling, or might do, a power known as mentalizing.

Humans aren't telepathic creatures, but we're pretty good at mind reading. A human toddler can intuit the actions or thoughts of people around him better than an adult of any other primate species. Isn't that wild? So if our brains have evolved to mentalize, dedicating thousands of hours to this ability, we must get a tremendous benefit from thinking about other people's thinking. Though it has its downsides, this obsession with one another, and ourselves, isn't a curse. It makes us more empathetic and more cooperative with the group. So why are we so hard on ourselves for revisiting an awkward social interaction at work when we're driving home? For spending hours hypothesizing whether a date will text us back?

"The great gift of the conscious brain," writes evolutionary biologist David Sloan Wilson in his book *This View of Life,* "is the capacity—and with it the irresistible inborn drive—to build scenarios." Scenarios about what might upset your family. What might win the boss's approval. What you might talk about with Beyoncé when she invites you to her house. Obviously, some of these are more useful than others.

In addition to making sense of others, humans can also think about our own thinking, a skill known as "metacognition." A dog cannot tell himself, "After much internal debate, I have determined what it means to be a good boy." He simply repeats what gets him a head pat and a piece of cheese. But humans can determine our convictions and try to live them out. We are both mind readers *and* mind knowers. Mind reading helps drive the togetherness force, and mind knowing reflects individuality at work.

One way to increase your own maturity, or level of differentiation, is to work on becoming more of a mind knower in your day-to-day life. Most of us don't need to practice mind reading—the default network will take care of that. But determining your own thoughts and beliefs is a muscle that must be exercised. This is the beginning of the shift from pseudo-self to solid self.

Because Margaret had moved into a new community, it made sense that her mentalizing powers were hard at work.

She imagined scenario after scenario of how her husband might embarrass her in front of new friends, or how she might piss off the neighbors. But she also needed to add her own thinking to the mix. How did she want to represent herself in these new relationships? How did she want to treat people? How did she want to spend her time?

Margaret was also highly tuned in to her children's ideas of who she should be. She'd never considered how she wanted to be a mother to adult children. Perhaps now was the time. Margaret tried to catch herself when she was thinking about others' reactions, and shift back to her own thoughts. Here's what it looked like:

MIND READING: I wonder if I hurt my son's feelings by not taking his advice.

MIND KNOWING: Do I think I was respectful but honest in our conversation?

MIND READING: Does my youngest son want me to call and check up on him?

MIND KNOWING: What kind of contact do I want to have with him?

MIND READING: Do the neighbors hate me for bringing up politics?

MIND KNOWING: Did I think it was a useful time to share my beliefs?

MIND READING: I shouldn't speak up because these people are smarter than me.

MIND KNOWING: How much did I let my anxiety dictate my participation?

Over time, Margaret began to talk differently about her relationships. Her challenges felt lighter and even humorous at times, because they were more interesting. After reflecting on one of Paul's lectures about exercise, she told me what a treasure he was. "What would I do if I didn't have anyone to spar with in the family? My relationship with him keeps me accountable; it's a place to be more of a self." To me, this is evidence that mind knowing isn't a stone-cold indifference toward others' feelings. A person who is less anxious to please may often be in a better position to empathize and listen thoughtfully.

Margaret also tried to stop lending her thinking to Grant when he fought with his ex-wife. She tried to be curious about his thinking, even in moments of high stress. She defined her job as staying connected to her son and grandkids in challenging times. By working on being a less anxious presence in their lives, she didn't have to fluctuate between accommodation and avoidance.

As far as her faith, Margaret wasn't thinking about leaving the Catholic church anytime soon. But she was starting to ask more questions out loud, and she set aside solo time to flesh out her beliefs. She paused before she repeated a prayer or recited a confession, considering whether the words were true for her. If not, she left them out or edited them.

Back at Friendship Village, Margaret began to see opportunities where she'd once seen social landmines. These new relationships were a chance for Margaret to represent herself and let her husband do the same. She made an effort to learn about people's beliefs and interests. But she also looked for opportunities to say, "I think about that differently," or "No, thanks, I'll pass," when the lawn bowlers edged over. To her surprise, no one snubbed her at the baked potato bar.

It was interesting to hear Margaret describe getting to know herself better. She learned that she had more of a backbone than she realized—one built by thirty-five years of relating to teenagers. She learned her youngest son could navigate an intense challenge with more self than she assumed. She saw how her oldest son could back off when she made her own decisions. She also learned that her new neighbors were more welcoming than she had imagined they'd be. There was less need to mind-read when you gave people opportunities to represent themselves.

Building a more solid self does not make for a lonely life. The more clarity we have in our thinking, the more genuine our relationships can be. And the less likely we are to anxiously inch away from people with different beliefs. It is incredibly rewarding to live a life where people know what we're about. A life where we look forward to getting to know ourselves.

EXERCISE 1: **Sensing togetherness.** Have you been a part of a group that's high in togetherness? A sorority in college? An anxious workplace? Your own family? Write down some of the characteristics that made it very together-ish. When have you been in a group with a better balance of togetherness and individuality? Where people were free to direct themselves and operate flexibly, but also accomplish goals together? Write down some of the characteristics that you think made it more balanced.

EXERCISE 2: **Your belief buffet.** Write down a few beliefs that you've adopted from your family or other sources. What beliefs were in conflict with one another? For example, maybe you believed that everyone is beautiful as they are, but you personally had to reach a certain weight to be valued. Circle the beliefs that crumbled, or would crumble, if and when you applied your own reasoning to them.

EXERCISE 3: **A day of mentalizing.** On a particular day, try to make a note anytime you're guessing what others are thinking or feeling. How many times did you do this? When/where were you vulnerable to mind reading? Mentalizing isn't bad—it's essential to group living! But consider when it is necessary to direct yourself toward mind knowing. What are upcoming opportunities to focus more on representing yourself and your beliefs the way you'd like?

CHAPTER NUGGETS

- Our ability to conform to the group is central to human cooperation and survival.
- Humans have a strong drive to determine our own thoughts and actions as well as a strong drive to think and act like others. In Bowen theory, these forces are called individuality and togetherness.
- When relationships and groups are high in togetherness, relationship pressure has a greater influence on people's decisions and beliefs.
- When individuality and togetherness are more balanced, there is more flexibility and openness in relationships. It is easier to make decisions based on your own thinking.
- Our brains are programmed to trust the intelligence of the group over individual thinking. The hormone oxytocin promotes conformity within the group.
- Many of our beliefs were borrowed from our relationship systems. Beliefs that are negotiable based on others' reactions are known as the pseudo-self.
- The solid self is comprised of beliefs that can survive relationship pressure and only change when you are presented with new evidence or experiences.
- Humans have the remarkable ability to mentalize, or make guesses about what others are thinking or feeling. The brain dedicates much of its time to making sense of our complex social living.
- Being a mind knower, rather than just a mind reader, is one way to work on differentiation. Developing your own beliefs can help you be less susceptible to relationship pressure.

4

HOW WE END UP OVERFUNCTIONING FOR OTHERS

"I decorated! I cooked! I made it nice!"
—Dorinda Medley, *The Real Housewives of New York City*

SUSAN'S MOTHER, MAUREEN, called her every hour on the hour. The *Today* show had a big makeover reveal. The photo wouldn't attach to the email. There were no more Oatmeal Creme Pies in the cupboard. The crabby neighbors had stopped by, furious that her leaves were falling into their pristine yard. Could Susan also hear a helicopter on her side of town? No, wait, it was just the leaf blower. Speaking of leaves, did she want to save her fourth-grade nature project? She had worked so hard on it, and it would be a pity to throw out.

Reader, it was relentless.

Susan's father had died from a heart attack at the age of seventy-five. Before his death, Susan hadn't considered how much her dad did for her mom. They'd always been a happy pair, an electrician and his chatty wife who gave piano lessons in their living room. Maureen had mastered Chopin and Stravinsky, but she never drove on the interstate, cooked anything more complicated than scrambled eggs, or paid the bills. At seventy-four, there were more than a few gaps in her own maturity. But they'd never created much anxiety, until her husband wasn't around to pick up the slack.

Distress is contagious, especially in a family. If you don't believe me, clearly you've never helped a parent fix their iPhone settings remotely. This sensitivity is annoying but necessary. Social mammals need to be able to sense stirrings in the group. A dog's levels of the stress hormone cortisol will rise if their human is crying. Prairie dogs listen for the furious foot thumping of their neighbors, warning them to leap back into their burrows.

In an anxious family, all we hear are thumps. Even more so after a death. Allergic to one another's distress, we activate those familiar patterns to keep things calm. This is how seemingly reasonable people end up fighting over a parent's estate. Why people remarry quickly to steady themselves. Anxiety increases relationship orientation and kicks the emotional process into gear. We become less creative, more caught up in rigid, automatic responses.

Susan was no exception to this rule. She needed someone to steady her after her father's death. She claimed her mother was a nuisance, but Maureen was a convenient focus. Susan quickly shifted into her father's role, lending her mother her own capabilities. And her mother was happy to borrow them. This pattern of lending and borrowing self, known in Bowen theory as "over- and underfunctioning," is one pattern a system uses to manage anxiety. (You've already learned about another in chapter 1—conflict.) Bowen used it to describe how one spouse can appear capable and the other dysfunctional, even if they are the same level of differentiation. But over- and underfunctioning is present in many types of relationships, whether it's mother and daughter, two colleagues, or two friends.

OVERFUNCTIONING GIVES YOU PSEUDO-STRENGTH

Imagine you followed Susan and Maureen around the grocery store as they searched for those elusive Oatmeal Creme Pies. If I asked you, "Who is the more mature person?" you'd probably point to Susan. And if I asked you, "Who's the less mature person?" you might point to her mother. This assessment ignores what is happening in the relationship system. Because they both have their own flavor of immaturity. Each was using the relationship pattern of over- and underfunctioning to prevent or manage tension.

Both the overfunctioner and underfunctioner benefit to some degree from the dynamic. Just like her father, Susan gained a pseudo-maturity, or pretend strength, from her position as the over-responsible one. Being in charge of her mother felt less stressful than letting her flail a little. In return, Maureen had everything done for her and her worries eased. Like a sea anemone hitching a ride on a hermit crab, their symbiosis gave them some level of protection they wouldn't have had otherwise.

Unfortunately, there is a hidden cost to over- and underfunctioning. An underfunctioner is more vulnerable to feeling and acting helpless when someone is always ready to swoop in and solve their problems. They might experience

Overfunctioning

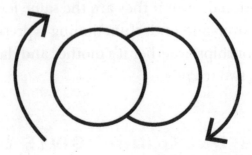

Underfunctioning

Figure 3. Over- and underfunctioning. The overfunctioner (left) lends self, and the underfunctioner (right) borrows self. The relationship may become calmer, but also less flexible.

physical symptoms, substance use problems, or other challenges. In turn, the overfunctioner may become more sensitive to the other's distress. They cannot tolerate watching the underfunctioner work on their own capability. Stuck in the over-responsible position, they're riding a runaway train toward burnout, which can lead to their own mental, physical, or emotional symptoms. So the dynamic works, until it doesn't. At some level of stress, symptoms will emerge.

If you're the oldest child in your family, or you acted like one, congratulations! You're more likely to overfunction for others. Do your mood or functioning get a boost when people need you? Health care professionals, educators, clergy, or other people in leadership roles may find that their mood, energy level, or abilities increase when they can be the comforter, the expert, or the shepherd. It can be useful to ask yourself, "How much of my supposed maturity relies on the way that people see me?"

SIGNS OF PSEUDO-MATURITY:

- Only feeling comfortable when you're in charge.
- Needing to be the expert.
- Wanting to speak for other people.
- Only being interested in things you can control.
- Functioning/mood dip when you're not in charge.

As someone in a helping profession . . . I feel you. I'm the only child of an oldest daughter. I'm most comfortable running the show. When I'm not in charge, or told to follow instructions, my immaturity can creep out. If I'm not careful, I'm likely to become overly critical, begin to underfunction, or check out completely. Therefore, not being in charge is an incredibly useful practice for me. It's an opportunity to ask, "What does being a responsible *participant* look like?"

Susan thought about how the pattern of over- and under-functioning played out in the multigenerational, emotional history of her family. A practice that helped was creating a family diagram, one of the most important tools in Bowen theory. Creating a diagram helps you record the facts of the family (or an organization) and its functioning across several or many generations. You get a better sense of what people were up against, and the patterns that emerged to manage tension. You begin to see how some people were more vulnerable to getting caught up in these patterns. If you're interested in creating your own family diagram, I've included a couple of resources at the end of this book. Obviously, it is a privilege to have access to information about previous generations in the family, an advantage that not everyone has. For those without access to multigenerational facts, any effort that can help you look at the functional facts (the who, what,

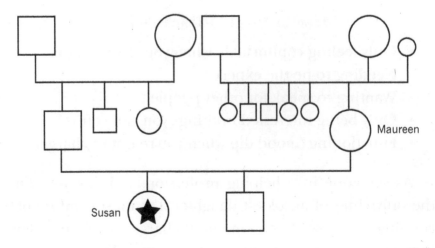

Figure 4. The family diagram. A typical family diagram would include much more information, including facts, dates, symptoms, and relationship patterns. Notice, however, how this simple diagram can expand your thinking about Susan and Maureen's relationship.

where, when, and how) of significant people in your life is likely to be worthwhile. Visual representations of facts and patterns in the system steer us away from "why" questions, which tend to rely on simple, cause-and-effect explanations.

Looking at her family diagram helped Susan not lose sight of the system when she talked about her relationship with her mom. She thought about how her father gained pseudo-maturity when he took care of her mother. And her mother was in a perfect position to be the underfunctioner in the marriage. Maureen was the youngest of six children. Her own mother (Susan's grandmother) was in and out of hospitals when Maureen was young. She died of cancer when Maureen was thirteen, and Maureen's siblings had passed their baby sister back and forth. They worried a lot about her, rarely treating her like she was capable. Once Susan's great-aunt told her she'd felt such relief when Maureen found an oldest son to marry. Clearly there was more at play here than a mother acting too "needy."

By seeing the patterns, Susan gave herself a greater chance of stepping outside them. Susan was not doomed to her sibling position. And Maureen could be more than the baby sister who needed a lot of help. But Susan had to think about how to untangle herself a little from the emotional process. How could she figure out what was hers to manage, and what wasn't? She would benefit from bringing a little more solid self to the family challenges.

THE MANY WAYS WE OVERFUNCTION

Of all the patterns we use to manage tension, the over-functioning and underfunctioning dynamic is perhaps the easiest to spot in your day-to-day life. For those who want to overfunction less, start with simple observation. Move throughout your day, paying attention without necessarily changing any behaviors. Ask yourself, "What do I do for others that they can do for themselves?"

This is not a call to abandon kindness. Overfunctioning is less about the content of our actions and more about the process. Are you living out your beliefs? Or simply managing your own discomfort? When I'm scheduling dinner with friends, I don't choose the restaurant out of the kindness of my heart. I do it because I am deeply allergic to watching people slowly make a decision. Whoops!

If you're struggling to think of examples, let me overfunction for you with a list of ways we sometimes overfunction for others. Feel free to put a check next to the ones that feel familiar to you.

50 WAYS YOU MIGHT OVERFUNCTION FOR OTHERS

1. Making sure your partner doesn't stay up too late.
2. Peppering your emails with phrases like "no worries" to reassure others.
3. Making goals for people that they don't have for themselves.
4. Finishing people's sentences.
5. Lecturing people on how to be "healthier."
6. Giving advice to a distressed friend who hasn't asked for any.
7. Always making the plans for your friend group.
8. Lecturing someone on how to cook dinner when they've volunteered.
9. Reminding others that they should hurry up and book travel.
10. Doing something for your child that they can do for themselves.
11. Always updating your spouse about a kid's school news.
12. Always taking on tasks at work rather than teaching others to do them.
13. Keeping a schedule for your partner because they often forget appointments.
14. Being overly accommodating when people need to schedule a meeting.
15. Not sharing important beliefs to prevent making others anxious.
16. Telling people on the internet what they should think or how they should act.

17. Reminding someone to take their medicine.
18. Telling someone what to order.
19. Researching information for someone who can look it up.
20. Creating a secret alternative plan when you know someone will mess up.
21. Reminding your partner to call their family.
22. Guessing what someone is going to say rather than asking them.
23. Managing how your partner parents your children.
24. Explaining someone else's thinking to others when they're present.
25. Always updating your friends and family about people they could contact.
26. Putting food on someone's plate when they haven't asked for it.
27. Trying to host people in their own home.
28. Cleaning up after someone because you think they're doing it too slowly.
29. Giving someone directions when they are capable of finding their way.
30. Buying someone a self-help book you've recommended.
31. Doing something for someone after they've communicated they're capable.
32. Reminding a colleague about an upcoming due date they already know.
33. Talking to a doctor on behalf of someone who is capable of communicating.
34. Making decisions for an adult parent that they can make themselves.

35. Mind-reading the wishes of a family member without asking them.
36. Telling a driver when to stop, speed up, or turn.
37. Constantly checking in with someone who's agreed to take on a project.
38. Teaching your partner how to act around your friends/family.
39. Leaving instructions for a task a person could easily figure out themselves.
40. Furiously completing tasks for others when you feel bored, anxious, or distressed.
41. Reassuring people that everything is going to be all right.
42. Talking a lot to fill in the gaps and awkward pauses in conversations.
43. Urging people to follow your previous unsolicited advice.
44. Trying to convince someone that your thinking is right.
45. Automatically paying for something to calm someone down.
46. Taking over a group project that is coming together slowly.
47. Steering your child away from experiences that may result in failure.
48. Worrying about other people's responsibilities.
49. Always volunteering for the most challenging piece of a project.
50. What would you add to this list?

When you look at this list, I'd encourage you to think about process, not content. The goal is not to refrain from these specific actions. The goal is to see how these behaviors may reveal a seesaw in relationships. Are there opportunities to step back and let people surprise you? To learn how to tolerate discomfort as your child, your friend, or your colleague learns to be more responsible for themselves? When you see opportunities to step back, you can help a relationship begin to function with less fusion and more flexibility, with less togetherness and more individuality.

Susan created her own list of behaviors with her mother that she wanted to change. Whenever Susan visited, she was either scrubbing the bathroom, doing meal prep, or opening the mail for a woman who didn't have any physical or cognitive challenges. And her mother was no bystander to the dynamic. She had a mental list ready when Susan arrived. When Susan asked her to do something, she'd make some fantastic excuse. Susan thought about how her flurry of anxious helping filled the empty space in their relationship, the space where there might have been good conversation, laughter, or even some arguments. There was no time to relate when there was so much to be done.

COACHING AND CRUISE DIRECTING

Susan's overfunctioning wasn't limited to her relationship with her mother. She spent a lot of energy telling her younger brother, Steven, how to relate to their mom. She'd call him with updates, and he felt less of a need to call Maureen. When she asked Steven to take Maureen to doctor's appointments, Susan would send pages of instructions and questions for him to ask the doctor. He'd successfully avoided their mother's yard-obsessed neighbors, because Susan wanted to handle it. There was no incentive to step up when his older sister always swatted him down. Susan had written Steven off as a slacker, but she was beginning to see her part in his underfunctioning. There was a reciprocity there that couldn't be denied.

Susan also found ways to overfunction at work. She enjoyed mentoring new employees, showing them how to navigate office drama and the boss's angry moods. But her own productivity took a hit when she directed her energy this way. By always playing a kind of coach in her relationships, Susan could avoid having to be in the game. She could evade the vulnerability that came with being herself and letting others do the same.

When we're always coaching others, the people we are coaching start to take their eyes off the game. They stop thinking about how they want to manage themselves, because you're doing it for them. In baseball, it's wise to let a third-base coach decide if you should speed up, slow down, or hightail it back to second base. But what works in baseball is not sustainable in our families or at work. No one becomes more responsible when they're being directed from the coach's box.

Overfunctioning also looks like playing cruise director in our relationships. We want people to have fun, feel comfortable, and avoid distress. Sometimes we do this because we love them, but sometimes it's because their distress is contagious. This is how we end up trying our damnedest to host the perfect party or plan the ideal trip. Why we jump in to fill the awkward silences or tell people what to order at a restaurant. We can expend a lot of energy bulldozing discomfort, creating an enjoyable, obstacle-free path for those around us. Whether it's protecting our kids from disappointment, minimizing the odds of family arguments, or giving our friends the perfect evening.

Susan was an expert cruise director. In her friendships, she spent so much of her energy planning gatherings and managing everyone. If a friend wasn't enjoying herself at a restaurant Susan had chosen, she'd spend the whole evening apologizing. If she noticed someone couldn't relate to a conversation topic, she'd steer it in a new direction. And when she wasn't in charge of a trip or a birthday gathering, her anxiety would skyrocket. She'd start to hound the leader with texts and emails, requesting and critiquing logistics, and then grow frustrated when they didn't comply. It was too easy to focus on her friends' shortcomings, wondering why they couldn't be thoughtful in similar ways. Rather than respecting her friends as individuals, she was treating them like an extension of herself. Just like she'd done with her mother.

So much of what we label as thoughtfulness has much more to do with anxious overfunctioning. Are we really thinking of others, or simply using these relationships to calm ourselves down?

BEING RESPONSIBLE *TO* PEOPLE, NOT *FOR* PEOPLE

Stepping back from overfunctioning is an important part of differentiation. But it's only a part. You can't just throw your hands in the air and shout, "Good luck, peasants! I'm out!" This is just anxious avoidance disguised as maturity.

After you step back, you need to step *up*. You learn to be part of a relationship, while also functioning as a more separate individual. In this case, Susan wanted to be more connected to her family and friends but less trapped in predictable patterns. To be a little more of a self in all her relationships.

Students of Bowen theory talk about being responsible *to* people rather than responsible *for* them. The simple change of a preposition can alter how you think about relating to a parent, a child, or a good friend. About what it means to be present and accounted for in a relationship, without overstepping. This opens up a new set of behaviors that replace being over-responsible for others. Because growing up is not just a thought experiment; differentiation is all about action—observable ways we can more thoughtfully relate to other humans.

ACTING RESPONSIBLE FOR SOMEONE OFTEN LOOKS LIKE:

- Assuming you know what they think.
- Trying never to upset them.
- Instantly dropping everything to help them.
- Trying to manage their distress.
- Telling them how to function.
- Teaching others how to interact with them.
- Discouraging their independent functioning.

BEING RESPONSIBLE TO SOMEONE COULD LOOK LIKE:

- Being curious about their thinking.
- Being honest about your interests, beliefs, and challenges.
- Showing up for important events.

- Letting them know when something isn't okay.
- Respecting the boundaries they set.
- Being responsible for managing your own distress.
- Letting others be in charge of themselves.
- Promoting their independent functioning.

Obviously, your responsibilities will vary depending on the age and abilities of the other person. Being responsible to an aging parent with Alzheimer's might look different from being responsible to a parent who's very independent. Being responsible to a sixteen-year-old will look different than being responsible to a five-year-old.

Susan began to think about what it might look like to be responsible *to* her mother. It looked less like wiping Popsicle juice off the remote, or raking the neighbor's yard in the dead of night. It looked more like stopping and listening when her mom began to tell her a story about Susan's grandmother. Like driving her to senior computer classes instead of barking IT instructions over the phone. It looked like telling her mom about her week, the joys, the challenges, all of it, whether her mother cared or could relate to the experiences of a forty-five-year-old single woman.

Susan also wanted to stop being over-responsible for her brother, Steven, and her friends. Rather than appreciating their individual differences, she'd expected them all to behave like she did. Differences were seen as deficits, rather than pluses. This had stifled any kind of authentic connection in the relationships. There was no energy to listen to a friend's challenges when Susan was wondering whether they liked their dessert. There was no time to hear how her brother was dealing with their dad's death when she was constantly giving him instructions. If she could focus less of her anxious energy on her loved ones, she could begin to give them her real attention.

Of course, none of this was easy. Interrupting what's automatic, and relating to someone without the boost of being in the driver's seat, can feel intensely alien. After all, the only thing harder than fixing your parents' Wi-Fi is watching them try to do it themselves. Watching your friend date a consulting bro, or letting your boss run an absolute dumpster fire of a meeting, is not fun. You'd like to think that stepping back grants instant lightness and freedom. But initially, you're likely to feel more weighed down with anxiety. Anxiety you now have to acknowledge and manage in a more mature way.

Over time, however, you may notice that your relationships do feel lighter and more genuine. And the moments you choose to step up begin to feel more meaningful. Susan could buy some extra cookies at the store because she loved her mother. Not because she felt obligated to do so. She could plan an amazing weekend with her friends, but then let people engage with those plans how they wished. Susan could be true to herself without telling other people who to be. Her generosity and attention to detail could be gifts to her relationships, not restraints that tied them down.

PUT DOWN YOUR ENNEAGRAM CHART FOR A HOT MINUTE

"Overfunctioning" is an increasingly popular term in the pop psychology world. When people talk about the behavior, they often treat it like a personality trait. Another quirky characteristic to add to your Instagram bio, like being an introvert, or an Enneagram number 3. We love labels that make us feel special. So it's no surprise that personality testing is a billion-dollar industry. But an individualized definition of overfunctioning fails to capture the reciprocity, the mutual corresponding actions, in our relationships. You can't have overfunctioning without an underfunctioner, someone who accepts or even invites the overinvolvement.

When we label ourselves as "overfunctioners," we overlook all the ways we underfunction in our relationships. We also miss that these patterns may change or fluctuate in their intensity. People are born and die in a family, circumstances evolve, and the level of anxiety ebbs and flows. When we label ourselves, we miss out on the complexity of the system. And our big brains were designed for that complexity. Part of learning to apply systems thinking is teaching oneself to ask *how* rather than *why*. Asking "Why?" only invites simple cause-and-effect answers to complex questions. It starts and ends with you saying, "I am this way because my mother did that."

Let me suggest an experiment. The next time you feel exhausted from socializing, focus less on the belief that you're an introvert. This might be true, but you also may have been interacting with a group that invited your overinvolvement. If you're a woman who's exhausted from emotional labor at home, you can certainly blame the patriarchy, which plays a part. But also consider what other variables create a vulnerability to being overinvolved. Maybe the anxiety is up. Maybe your spouse tends to distance when they're distressed. Perhaps you're also an oldest child in your family. This isn't about excusing people's actions or societal problems. And it's not about blaming yourself. Instead it's an attempt to see how the system works when it's easy to reach for a single explanation or villain. To see how the Ferris wheel turns and what opportunities there may be to hop off the ride. To redirect your energy toward a more productive outlet—yourself. Systems thinking keeps us from saying, "That's just the way I am." It creates curiosity, and even hope, when it's all too easy to feel stuck.

TURNING BURDENS INTO GIFTS

Susan was ready to change her part in her relationships, and she decided to begin her work with her friends. Her first task was to pull back on the cruise directing and show up when others were gathering. When someone chose a bad restaurant for dinner, she ate a big lunch and went anyway. When she sensed somebody was bored by the conversation, she reminded herself that they could change the topic. When nobody could pick a vacation destination to save their life, she tried to be patient and observe as the system reoriented itself. Their cruise director had retired, and the friend group needed some time to readjust. Would a new overfunctioner emerge, or would the group begin to share responsibility more equally? Either way, Susan had changed her part.

Susan also tried to see her younger brother, Steven, as a capable human. When she asked him to help with Maureen, she tried not to give intensely specific directions. He was flummoxed by this. He began to act less capable in the short term, to re-invite her overfunctioning. "Mom can tell you what she needs" became her go-to reply. Susan was still contact number one on her mother's ancient landline, but she began to suspect that Steven was getting more of the action.

By pulling back on her coaching, Susan had helped Steven's relationship with Maureen, her relationship with Maureen, and her relationship with Steven all become more flexible. She didn't need to be the operator that connected everyone or translated every need.

Now came the fun part. Armed with a long list, Susan knew there were a million opportunities to interrupt her overfunctioning at her mother's house. She realized that Maureen wouldn't die if she scrambled eggs two nights in a row or watched two hours of *Murder, She Wrote*. She could play an out-of-tune piano for a week or two, or ask Steven to unlock her Facebook account. Rather than acting like a twenty-four-hour hotline, Susan called her mother at 6 P.M. every evening on her way home from work. Though it felt strange at first, she tried to ask questions about her mother's life. Questions about the past, what she wanted from the future, and what was challenging about having your spouse die first. She learned that curiosity is a byproduct of asking good questions, not a prerequisite.

Maureen didn't become super-responsible overnight. She still hid in the bathroom when the leaf-obsessed neighbors knocked on her door (who wouldn't?). Her first instinct when the smoke detector batteries went out, or the Little Debbies were dangerously low, was to call Susan. But Susan was beginning to feel less reactive when she was summoned. She could tell her mother it wasn't a good time to talk. When it was a good time, she could be more present. Perhaps one day, she could even provide tech support without losing her ever-loving mind. Dream big, kids.

Little by little, the seesaw was tilting more evenly. In a stressful week, Susan would easily shift into her anxious fixing. The emotional process is a powerful thing, and it takes a lot of practice to function with more self. But Susan had the rest of her life to tinker with the challenges. Every relationship was an opportunity to operate with a little more self and to respect the individuality of others. As long as her mother was alive, Susan knew that their relationship would be the best and hardest place for Susan to become a little more grown up. What she had once called a burden was now a real gift. And she wasn't planning on wasting it.

EXERCISE 1: **Seeing the seesaws.** Look at the last few generations in your family. Where do you see evidence of over- and underfunctioning? How did the overfunctioners benefit from this position? How did they not? For better or worse, how did this pattern stabilize the family to some degree? Now look at your generation. Who was the most susceptible to falling into this pattern? If you or your siblings have kids, who might be next?

EXERCISE 2: **Overfunctioning scavenger hunt.** To interrupt overfunctioning, you have to practice observing it. Turn on your favorite TV show, go to a family or friend gathering, or pay attention at your next big work meeting. How many times do people overfunction for others in their behaviors or language? How do some people invite this overfunctioning from others? Who becomes a coach or a cruise director? Observation helps us be less judgy when humans act predictably under stress. It also highlights the opportunities to do something different.

EXERCISE 3: **Being responsible *to* someone.** Are there relationships in your life where you could work on being responsible *to* people rather than *for* them? What might it look like to relate to these people without overfunctioning for them? Do you need to share more about your own life? Sit on your hands when you're tempted to take over? Think of two upcoming opportunities where you can practice being present without anxiously taking over.

CHAPTER NUGGETS

- Humans are built to sense one another's distress. Increase the anxiety, and you increase the level of relationship orientation.
- People often borrow or lend "self" to manage the anxiety in a relationship system. This can create a seesaw effect, a pattern known as overfunctiong and underfunctioning.
- Overfunctioners can gain a kind of pseudo-maturity, or pretend strength, by being over-responsible for others. But they do risk burnout or other symptoms when this pattern becomes too rigid, or as stress increases.
- A family diagram, which captures the facts and functioning of a family (or organization) across the generations, is a useful tool for systems thinking and working on differentiation. This tool helps steer people away from simple cause-and-effect explanations we tend to use in our relationships.
- If you pay attention to overfunctioning in your day-to-day life, you will find opportunities to step back and let others be responsible for themselves.
- One way we overfunction is by coaching others on how to navigate their relationships. Another is to play cruise director, overplanning and removing any obstacles that might cause distress.
- A person working on greater maturity (differentiation of self) can benefit from thinking about how

they want to be responsible *to* people, rather than responsible *for* people.

- Overfunctioning is not a personality trait. It is one part of a reciprocal pattern where both the over-functioner and the underfunctioner participate. A person may over- and underfunction in different arenas of life.

5

HOW WE END UP UNDERFUNCTIONING

"We can! We will! We must!"
> —the Navarro College cheerleaders

EVERYONE LOVED LUIS. Sure, he was often late to work. Yes, he was a little behind with his credit card payments. When you told him to pick you up at Dulles, he might show up at Reagan instead. But his sunny, encouraging personality made him easy to forgive. His husband, Drew, was attracted to his go-with-the-flow attitude, one he'd never been able to summon himself. What was once endearing, however, was now putting great strain on their marriage.

Meeting Drew was like finding the personal assistant Luis never had. Drew was organized. He arrived at the airport three hours early. He unironically hung his personal goals on the refrigerator, and he made the coffee before Luis woke up. It was like being married to an Excel spreadsheet who went to the gym five days a week. And it was glorious.

Opposites attract, and so do over- and underfunctioners. At first the pattern was a comfortable fit, causing very little trouble for the couple. But dial up the stress, and the adaptive dynamic began to feel suffocating. During a stressful year at work, Drew began to work longer hours. Then his mother was diagnosed with cancer, and he had to drive home on the weekends. Drew told Luis he needed to be more responsible for himself. But he kept overfunctioning for Luis, this time with great resentment. Sensing the rising distress in his partner, Luis felt paralyzed. He couldn't seem to step up, and he couldn't understand why.

THE CASE OF THE DISAPPEARING MAN

People in happy marriages often say their spouse makes them a better person. But marriage also can make us spectacularly incapable. When you get married, you get a pretty good deal. Bills are magically paid. The car has gas in it. Clean clothes migrate back to your closet. Someone else can listen to your Aunt Beverly talk about *The Masked Singer.* Marriage frees up energy for other endeavors. But there can be a hidden cost. When you don't exercise certain muscles of responsibility, they begin to atrophy.

If you're married or cohabitate, what would you do as a single person that now feels like a burden? Taking out the trash used to feel very easy to me. But if I have to do it now, I act like I should get the Presidential Medal of Freedom. I am aware of my capability, but the urge to "borrow self" is very strong. Why talk to another human on the phone when someone else can do it? Why learn the names of the kids in your child's class when your partner already knows them? Why go downstairs to get a glass of water when your spouse, who is already very comfortable in bed, has legs? It's fascinating to see how wimpy we become when you toss in another person.

Living with Drew had impacted Luis's functioning. While his financial security increased, thanks to Drew's advice on retirement, his growth in financial literacy had stalled. Once confident in his fashion choices, Luis now relied on Drew's compliments or silences when choosing an outfit. Drew also did all the research when they planned a trip, bought a car, or declared war on the neighborhood rats. Luis was getting to work on time. He was less likely to eat McDonald's three days in a row. But the relationship had interrupted some of the grown-up learning he might have accumulated as a single person.

WE BORROW SELF WHEN WE ALWAYS LET OTHERS:

- Navigate while we drive.
- Reassure us excessively.
- Be a buffer when we meet new people.
- Decide we need to go to the doctor.
- Deal with upset children.
- Talk to a difficult family member for us.
- Learn a new technology and then teach us.
- Remember where we parked.
- Make a phone call for us.
- Decide whether we look good or not.
- Manage finances without us.
- Decide what our goals are.
- Decide what we believe.

How have you borrowed self in a relationship with a partner, a friend, or a family member? Responsibilities can and must be shared in any relationship. We all have gifts and interests that influence what we do. But I'm not talking about the thoughtful division of labor. Over- and underfunctioning is the automatic, emotionally driven seesaw that occurs in any relationship to some degree. The ways we use others to fill our own maturity gaps.

GETTING HIGH OFF THE GROUP

Humans are also masters at borrowing self from our groups. Because we are deeply social, we love a group. We love them so much we pay real money to be locked in rooms and escape together. We'll take up a sport we secretly loathe, just to be around other humans. I'd never want to be a part of a cult like NXIVM, but I would like someone to invite me to midnight volleyball. I think it has a lot to do with my evangelical childhood, where an enthusiastic welcome, the right chord progressions, and oversharing in casual conversation created a cozy togetherness. Or my time in internet fandom, where the possibility of two fictional people banging produces a frenzied, warlike nation of fans.

Groups make us feel good, and they can also make us more productive. If your team just won the Super Bowl, or your favorite TV couple just kissed, you might experience a burst of productivity. In one fascinating study, researchers had participants working individually on a puzzle. One group of individuals was given clues that they were working on the puzzle with a team, and the other was not. The individuals who thought they were on a team (even though there weren't other people in the room) spent almost 50 percent more time on the puzzle. They also reported being more interested in the task. Without even being physically together! This the power of psychological togetherness.

Born into a big Salvadoran family, Luis was drawn to the energy of the group. When he was a kid, his family attended a fundamentalist church where members bonded over their fear of "worldly influences." Luis's mom had struggled with depression, and she used groups to boost her functioning. She would hop in and out of weight loss programs or multilevel marketing organizations, but these groups took a huge bite out of her bank account. Luis's dad was quick to overfunction for her. He kept a steady job, and treated his wife like she couldn't be trusted to manage their kids. Luis remembered his father calling in grandmas and aunts to pick up the slack. No wonder his mother had sought confidence from other groups.

Luis inherited his mother's love of togetherness. In high school, Luis joined the marching band, riding the highs and lows of competition. Band kept Luis on track for college where he served as a residential advisor. In the dorm, he'd gather all his "babies" together and help them with their feelings and challenges. At work, he was forever the office cheerleader. At the gym, he felt more motivated in group classes than when flying solo.

Just like individuals, groups can lend self. They can boost what Bowen called your "functional level of differentiation." Your functional level is how mature or capable you *appear* to be. Because the right environment, the right people, or the right words can make us appear quite capable.

GROUPS CAN LEND SELF BY:

- Telling you what your goals are.
- Telling you what to believe.

- Satisfying cravings for love and acceptance.
- Encouraging you when you aren't motivated.
- Create a temporary high through sharing thoughts/ feelings.
- Holding you accountable when you aren't performing.

Groups can provide us with a temporary boost in functioning. But this boost may disappear as soon as conflict arises or the group falls apart. Somewhere between these highs and lows is our basic level of differentiation—how mature we really are. Because we don't live in a vacuum, it's difficult to gauge how differentiated a person really is. Researchers have tried to create instruments to measure differentiation of self, but these only tell us so much. We are constantly gaining and losing functioning, depending on how others respond to us, how nice the weather is, or whether our favorite team is winning. But these influences don't make working on differentiation irrelevant; they make it more important. We can't control how others respond to us, but we can work on how we represent ourselves in relationships and life's challenges.

Luis didn't need to become a hermit to become more responsible for himself. He didn't need to abandon his relationships or even stop being an encourager. But Luis did need to think about how to generate energy that was less dependent on others' reactions. More than anything, he wanted to be surprised by his own capabilities.

MOVING PAST "MAT TALK"

In the early days of the COVID-19 pandemic, I watched the Netflix documentary *Cheer.* It's no surprise that the tenacious Navarro cheer team, a tight-knit squad achieving unbelievable physical feats, captivated a population stuck in isolation. Every person on the team was essential, including those off the mat, who encouraged their performing teammates with "mat talk." The phrase "mat talk" blasted across the pop psychology world, because who doesn't love being encouraged? Couldn't we all use some mat talk in our daily lives?

I found the docuseries inspiring, but I wondered what would happen to these young athletes after their days of competition were over. Would they experience the same rate of depression as returning military veterans or Peace Corps volunteers, struggling without the purpose and camaraderie they once shared?

It's useful to observe how teachers navigate the dilemmas with mat talk. Often a teacher will try to encourage without excessive praise. Instead of saying, "Good job!" they might say, "Look at this picture! Can you tell me about it?" Or, "Look what you were able to do!" Sometimes we're so focused on getting praise that we miss an opportunity to observe what we've been doing, and how we managed to do it. A chance to get curious about our behaviors and how we generate intrinsic motivation. Instead of telling myself, *Wow, queen! You did great today!* I might ask, *How did I manage to get into a good flow of work? What were the obstacles?* This allows the work itself to become the reward.

Luis was a fan of both getting and giving mat talk. He

loved receiving encouraging texts from friends. He always worked harder at the gym when someone was coaching him. But he also realized that these were temporary boosts. No amount of mat talk was going to shift his underfunctioning. Needing Drew to be in a peppy mood put too much pressure on the relationship. Relying on vibes at work put him at the mercy of his coworkers.

Luis began to think about what it might mean to move past mat talk toward more of what he called "prep talk," thinking that was less about judgment and more about curiosity and preparing for the challenges ahead. What was important or interesting to Luis, regardless of people's reactions?

Mat Talk	Prep Talk
You can do it!	How would I like to be responsible today?
Get it!	How would I define a good day?
You are worthy!	What's worth doing, even if nobody notices?
You are amazing!	What have I managed to pull off?
Nothing can stop you!	What are the challenges I might face?

Luis didn't need to change his personality. There are times when mat talk may be the best gift we can give ourselves and others. But there are other moments when asking a good question is the kindness we need. Finding the balance between the power of the group and the sweetness of the work itself is no easy thing. I suspect the Navarro cheer-leaders have figured this out better than I ever could.

ARE YOU A CONTENT CHASER?

We live in a world of unlimited self-improvement content. It's easy to find ideas, techniques, and motivation from books, podcasts, or social media when you need them. The industry we call self-help often has very little self in it at all. Because chasing after content can become another way we borrow self to ease our anxieties.

There's nothing wrong with consuming content. The trouble is, it's easy to get stuck in the consuming phase, where we think about changing, because it can *feel* like prog-ress. Maybe you love to listen to podcasts about goal setting. Or buying planners to record all your goals. Your brain can get a nice dose of dopamine from all these actions. Unfor-tunately, there's a huge chasm between the dopamine spike you get from setting a goal and the dopamine hit you get from being close to accomplishing the goal. And that gap is where a lot of the action must happen. You can read book after book about writing a novel, but one day you'll have to start typing. You can listen to a million podcasts about vulnerability, but at some point you have to open up to your friends.

The production and consumption of motivational con-tent is a pretty good measure for our level of anxiety as a society. Thanks to the internet, we spend a lot of energy try-ing to be gurus or trying to find them. Both are attempts to gain pseudo-maturity through our relationships. Part of my challenge as a therapist is not to fall into this trap. If I'm telling somebody how to solve their problems, or giving them excessive mat talk, it's likely a sign of my own undifferentiation—my inability to tolerate someone else's distress while they work on their challenges. I may overfunction because it feels good to be an "expert."

With all this borrowing and lending of self, there's little time left to know our own minds. And mind wandering is an essential part of creative problem-solving. Your brain needs time to make thoughtful connections so you can plan for the future or navigate life's challenges. But in the cult of productivity, it *feels* like we're doing more by watching an Instagram reel on personal growth than when we're sitting with our own thoughts.

Luis could look at his phone and see how he consumed content to feel motivated. There were podcasts with popular gurus. Fitness influencer accounts on Instagram. Ebooks on positivity and vulnerability. Upbeat playlists to keep the dopamine flowing. He didn't need to toss all his content. But he could pay attention to his consumption habits. Was he listening to a podcast to educate himself? Or to manage his anxiety and produce a temporary high?

Those moments when Luis wanted to hit play, or start scrolling, were opportunities to think without training wheels. So he tried waiting at the dentist's office without music in his ear. He walked to the store without constant, cheerful guidance. Getting comfortable with his own thoughts was an important part of working on differentiation. When Luis began to make space for his own thinking, he was one step closer to living it out.

STANDING UP TO OVERFUNCTIONERS

Learning to be more responsible for yourself is not a solo sport. Underfunctioning is part of a relationship pattern, a dance that depends on the overfunctioner. Luis looked at his parents' marriage and saw how his father had squashed his mother's attempts to become more responsible. But he also saw how his mother had invited the overinvolvement of his father. Luis also faced this challenge in his marriage with Drew. If so much of the anxiety in their marriage was managed through a pattern of over- and underfunctioning, interrupting this pattern would generate some tension. But in the long run, it would make the marriage more flexible and probably more fun.

When you've been underfunctioning, stepping up requires some courage. You might have to tell people you need them to back off and let you struggle a little. And you'll have to tell them more than once. As my husband says when I tell him how to cut a cantaloupe, "Kathleen, I'm a self." In those moments, I am both impressed and annoyed that I've been caught red-handed in my overfunctioning. I know that he is in the right, but I still feel injured. This is simply the tension felt when a dynamic is interrupted. It's what a person is up against when they want to change a relationship pattern. Feelings are going to be felt. That doesn't mean you're going in the wrong direction.

Here are some examples of what it can look like to stand up to overfunctioners.

GIVING IN: Letting someone finish your sentences.
STANDING UP: Telling them you would like to speak for yourself.

GIVING IN: Letting someone give you endless advice.
STANDING UP: Telling them you're not interested in advice at the moment.

GIVING IN: Letting someone mediate every squabble you have.
STANDING UP: Telling them you'd like to handle the conflict on your own.

GIVING IN: Letting someone give you directions while you're driving.
STANDING UP: Saying, "Look at me. I'm the captain now."

That last one was a joke, but you get the idea. Sometimes humor is the best way to share your thinking, and sometimes it isn't. And you don't always have to call people out for their overfunctioning. Sometimes an "I'm good, thanks" is all it takes. When you step up, sometimes people will draw back naturally, relieved that you've taken over. But there will be moments when you need to stand firm and speak up. Or as my child screams, "Mommy, I am Miss Independent!"

When someone overfunctions for you, it's easy to take it personally. But thinking about the emotional process helps us not play the blame game. Luis's problem wasn't that Drew didn't have faith in him. They were stuck in a pattern that was difficult for either of them to interrupt. The good news is that it would only take one of them to shake things up. The more Luis stepped up, the more Drew had evidence of his husband's capability. Or if Drew could thoughtfully step back, rather than angrily retreating, there would be space for change. Either way, the relationship gained more flexibility.

WHEN QUESTIONS HELP MORE THAN ANSWERS

Whatever the gurus may tell you, there is no single path to becoming a more mature version of yourself. This can be frustrating for people who are used to being told what to do. People get aggravated if you ask them, "What do you think is the best way forward?" Because they sense you have plenty of ideas. Whether you're somebody's therapist or friend, we can all ask questions about relationships that spark good thinking in others. Answers from others can calm distress, but they cannot help a person become more responsible for themselves.

HERE ARE A FEW QUESTIONS I ASKED LUIS:

- If you aren't paying attention in relationships, what happens?
- Where have you seen evidence of your lack of maturity?
- Where have you seen evidence of your growing maturity?
- What wisdom would you like to activate in tense situations?
- How do you want to represent yourself in your marriage? In other relationships?

These questions have no agenda. They are simply an attempt to stimulate thinking. People can have a hard time coming up with answers. When we are knee-deep in relationship orientation, we don't see ourselves as the way out of anything. We expect others to change, or a professional to tell us how to change. Or we simply want the immediate relief of venting our problems to a third party.

In her book about Bowen theory, *Extraordinary Relationships,* Roberta Gilbert wrote, "Differentiation is work done for self, by self." It is the work of a thousand trials and errors followed by small glimmers of maturity. It is being able to manage yourself amid these failures because your brain thinks differently about the problem—in a more curious and less critical way.

Luis started to define how he'd like to represent himself in his marriage. First, he wanted to dial down his reactivity when Drew complained about his underfunctioning. Rather than crying or escaping, he wanted to remember that Drew was reacting to the inflexibility, the stuckness, in the relationship. Luis didn't have to agree with everything Drew said, but he also didn't have to act as though he was on trial for murder. Second, he wanted to find small ways each day to bring a little more self to his actions. Whether it was letting his mind wander, setting his own alarm clock, or writing "DULLES" on the palm of his hand.

Luis didn't need to transform into a person who made it to the airport early or kept his closet organized. There can be as little self in those behaviors as there is in their opposites. Conformity to Drew wasn't the solution any more than playing Drew's opposite. Luis needed to be true to his own definition of a responsible, meaningful life. There were times when Luis stepped up, assembling furniture or making phone calls without asking Drew for help. But there were also times when Luis stood firm in his knowledge of himself, not fretting about the state of the house when friends came over, or having fun getting lost on a road trip. Choice by choice, he saw how the gap between his best thinking and his behaviors could shrink. As long as he kept asking himself, *Who do I want to be today?*, his brain would keep giving him answers. He didn't need to borrow them from anyone else.

EXERCISE 1: **Work those weak muscles.** Make a list of the skills you lost, or the skills you never built, because others were willing to function for you (e.g. driving, home maintenance, having difficult conversations). Circle three of the skills that you'd like to work on improving this year. How could these skills be beneficial in relationships where you've been more likely to underfunction?

EXERCISE 2: **Alternatives to mat talk.** Where in life do you rely on encouraging words from others to be responsible? What questions can you ask yourself before you automatically seek this reassurance (e.g. *How do I think I did? What do I think will be useful for me today?*). Everyone loves mat talk, but it doesn't have to be your only medicine. Sometimes it's just the icing on the cake.

EXERCISE 3: **Are you a content chaser?** Make a list of some of the self-help or motivational content you've consumed in the past year. Upon reflection, when were you more focused on getting that dopamine spike than working on your goals? How can you make more space in the week to let your mind wander and ask yourself good questions?

CHAPTER NUGGETS

- Everyone has maturity gaps in their own functioning; we often use our relationships to fill these gaps.

When we let others be over-responsible for us, we are underfunctioning.

- Other individuals or groups can boost our functioning and help us appear more mature or capable. How mature or immature you appear based on this boost is your functional level of differentiation.
- Your basic level of differentiation is how mature you really are, irrespective of relationship influences.
- We often rely on encouraging comments from others to boost our functioning. Generating curiosity and intrinsic motivation can help a person rely less on others' responses in order to function.
- Consuming content about self-improvement can activate the reward system in the brain, but it doesn't always make us more responsible for ourselves.
- Underfunctioners who want to become more responsible may experience pushback from the overfunctioner when they try to step up. This is an opportunity to learn to manage the inevitable anxiety that comes from disrupting a relationship pattern.
- Questions that help us assess our functioning (and define how we want to grow up) are often more helpful than answers we might borrow from others.

6

THE WAYS WE DISTANCE
FROM OTHERS

"I'm trying to elevate small talk to medium talk."
—Larry David, *Curb Your Enthusiasm*

WHEN SYLVIE WAS four years old, her family split in two. The chaos began when her paternal grandfather died. Three months after his funeral, Grandma Lynn shocked everyone by eloping with her dead husband's business partner. A blowout ensued over her grandfather's will, and Sylvie's father decided he was done with his mother and sisters, who didn't want much to do with him either. For the next twenty years, Sylvie's parents pretended that this side of the family had never existed.

Now Sylvie was twenty-seven. Her grandmother, more a myth than a person at this point, was somewhere in warm Arizona, chasing after great-grandchildren Sylvie had never met. Her absence was a manageable sadness, an artifact Sylvie's brain pulled out of storage on the holidays, or in therapy sessions. Until one day, when her father called to announce that he'd reconnected with Grandma Lynn. "Do you want to have a relationship with her again?" he asked.

Sylvie's body went into high alert. Her muscles tensed, her breathing grew rapid, and the tears were rolling. How could the prospect of chatting with a little old lady inspire such terror? She didn't even remember her grandmother. So why was her body preparing for war or retreat?

This is the power of the emotional process in a family. Avoiding Grandma had kept things calm, to a degree, in her nuclear family. Interrupting this pattern meant increasing the anxiety, at least in the short term. It's no surprise Sylvie's brain took one look at the situation and said, "I'm out."

THE MANY WAYS WE DISTANCE

Distance is a part of any relationship. Maybe you like your mother better when there's an ocean between you. Or you only talk to your brother about your fantasy football team. Maybe you look at your phone too much at dinner, or create an escape plan when you visit a talkative friend. Perhaps you're a millennial like me and would rather die than have someone pop by your house unexpectedly.

Distance is another relationship pattern used to manage anxiety. (You've already learned about two—conflict and over- and underfunctioning.) It's one way that we react to fusion in our relationships, the pressure to think and feel as one unit. Distance can be physical, but it can also be emotional. We create emotional distance when we hide our thinking, our beliefs, and our true selves from others. Differences in political beliefs aren't a problem if you never talk about them. Disapproval can be avoided if you never introduce your partner to your parents. If you never show your real self to people, you can escape the pain of being rejected. Even a chimpanzee will hide his nervous expression. Like us, he knows that revealing his cards would put him at risk.

Bowen theory refers to the most extreme form of distance as "cutoff," or "emotional cutoff." Sylvie's father had cut off his mother and siblings in the intensity following her grandfather's death, achieving some stability at a great cost. Cutoff can lower the reactivity in a family, but it does not address the degree of the fusion in relationships. You can still spend a lot of time thinking about and reacting to someone you never see.

Whether it's superficial conversation or intense cutoff, we all use distance to some degree to manage relationship tension.

DISTANCING COULD LOOK LIKE:

- Becoming very busy at work to avoid your family.
- Using alcohol or drugs to avoid sober conversations.
- Moving far away from your family.
- Only talking about sports or the weather.
- Canceling on people at the last minute to feel sweet, sweet relief.
- Texting someone when you should probably call them.
- Avoiding listening to an important voicemail.
- Always talking about your kids (and not yourself) with your spouse.
- Lying about your beliefs to avoid a disagreement.
- Only seeing your family on duty visits.

- Asking someone lots of questions to avoid sharing about your own life.
- Always ghosting dates instead of telling them you're not interested.
- Saying "I'm good" when you aren't.
- Changing the subject when you sense people are anxious.
- Not introducing yourself to people who seem cooler than you.
- Not initiating conversations with people who look different from you.
- Avoiding contact with people who are sick or dying.
- Not talking about family history that is anxiety producing.
- Bringing up a difficult topic during the last two minutes of therapy.
- Not engaging in conversations that are hard but important.
- Turning on the television at social gatherings.
- Double-booking so you have an easy out at a gathering.
- Planning nonstop fun to keep everyone busy.
- Assuming people aren't interested in your weird hobbies.
- Dismissing your accomplishments to make others comfortable.

Distance has its uses. At times, fleeing the room or changing the conversation may be the best way to navigate a sticky situation. Maybe you need to get clear about your thinking before you share it with someone. Maybe you need to end a relationship that is harmful. But some of the time, distancing is not a reflection of our best thinking. It is simply a pattern in the emotional process—a quick relief that comes with a cost.

WHEN WE ALWAYS MANAGE TENSION BY DISTANCING, WE LOSE OPPORTUNITIES TO:

- Build stronger one-on-one relationships.
- Work on our own maturity.
- Be responsible to the group.
- Define our thinking to others.
- Practice self-regulating our anxiety.
- Reduce our reactivity to others' distress.

Sylvie was a responsible person but also an expert at emotional distance. It was an emergency brake she couldn't release, even when she wanted to build stronger relationships. New to the city, she felt extremely anxious when meeting new people. After a night out, she'd lie in bed awake, replaying everything she'd said, worrying about how awkward she'd sounded to new acquaintances. She felt more comfortable with old friends, but these relationships also frustrated her. She was tired of dissecting the drama of *Love Island* episodes, sharing memes back and forth, or retelling the same stories from high school or college. But these relationships were better than nothing, so she let them stay stuck in the superficial.

CHRONIC ANXIETY
ENCOURAGES DISTANCE

Is there a high degree of emotional distance in your relationships? Do your relationships feel precarious, easily disturbed by stressful events? If so, there was probably a high level of chronic anxiety in your family of origin. Bowen defined "chronic anxiety" as the kind of anxiety generated by relationship tension. The more fused your family is, the more chronic anxiety it will have.

Chronic anxiety is different than the acute anxiety generated by short-term problems. Losing your job can create acute anxiety, but bracing yourself for your mother to panic about your unemployment? That's a sign of chronic anxiety. Showing up at the wrong restaurant when meeting a friend? Acute anxiety. Worrying this new friend thinks you're flaky—that's chronic anxiety. The latter often gets us into more trouble than the initial challenge because it keeps us stuck in relationship orientation, in an intense focus on others. It's how you waste a lot of energy trying to convince your mother that you'll be all right. Or showing your friend that you're actually the most responsible human on the planet.

AT HIGHER LEVELS OF CHRONIC ANXIETY, WE:

- Are more sensitive to people.
- Crave attention and approval.
- Become allergic to others' need for closeness.
- Spend a lot of time mind reading.
- Worry about others' reactions.
- Tend to find people more annoying.
- Tend to be less tolerant.

You can see all these reactions encourage overinvolvement with others, or the opposite reaction—distance. Chronic anxiety shuts down flexibility in relationships, and we end up smashing the same predictable buttons to keep things calm. *Attack! Take over! Give in! Give up! Run away!*

When chronic anxiety is high, people become more dependent on one another *and* more allergic to this dependence. It makes us go, "Help! No, not like that!" This happened in Sylvie's family after her grandfather's death. They wanted one another's support, but they were also more critical of how they provided this support (or didn't provide it). They also were less tolerant of the different ways people grieved the loss. Her grandmother's decision to remarry so quickly, and her dad's frustration with how the estate was handled, were reactions the system couldn't handle. And so the family fell apart. It shifted into a more rigid mechanism for managing the tension: total cutoff.

Cutoff is different from the well-reasoned choice to disconnect from a relationship. It is the relationship pattern used when a person or group of people is unable to tolerate the individuality of the other, when we expect people to do as we do, or have nothing to do with us. The third way of differentiation—connecting as individuals, flaws and all—does not feel feasible when chronic anxiety is high.

Given her family's emotional history, it's no surprise that Sylvie dedicated so much effort to keeping things peaceful. That she stayed in the shallow end of the pool when it came to conversations. But now she wondered if distance was worth the price. The cost of her family's calmness was high. She had lost a relationship with her only living grandparent, as well as aunts, uncles, and cousins. She felt lonely and anxious in a new city, and unsatisfied with the friendships she did have. She was ready to dive into the deep end, despite her body's initial reaction.

PERSON-TO-PERSON RELATIONSHIPS

Most of us don't want our relationships to stall in distant, superficial chatter. We crave relationships where we can talk about our beliefs and experiences, even if they are different. We want to be honest about how we're doing. We want to talk about what excites us without worrying about boring people. But creating these kinds of relationships with our friends or our family can be daunting.

Bowen theorized that developing person-to-person relationships was the best way for a person to become more mature, to work on differentiation of self. He outlined three key qualities for a person-to-person relationship.

1. Talking about your own beliefs and experiences.
2. Avoiding focusing on a third person.
3. Not relying on impersonal topics.

Developing a person-to-person relationship is about representing your authentic self to others, and letting others do the same. The more of a self you can be in your relationships, the easier it becomes to engage in meaningful conversation without feeling threatened or becoming defensive. This doesn't mean you share your dreams with Bob in accounting, or tell your sister that she looks horrible in that dress. Instead, it is a call to step outside our automatic functioning in relationships and summon the courage to be ourselves. To honor those competing drives to connect and operate as an individual.

Families, however, can be the toughest place to develop these kinds of relationships. You might have a person-to-person relationship with one parent and not the other. Maybe your sibling relationships rely on poking fun at parents. Adult grandchildren may present a superficial, squeaky-clean image to grandparents so they don't shock Grandma into an early grave. Where are opportunities to represent yourself more authentically in your relationships? To move toward people rather than away from them?

The more person-to-person relationships you have with everybody, the more flexibly the family can function. Increase the frequency of contact, and the quality of the contact, and you're going to have a higher functioning group, one where relationships are more open and authentic. If I have a problem with Uncle Joe, I can go to him, rather than asking my cousin to talk to my aunt about him. This thinking also applies in organizations, religious congregations, or any group working toward a goal. So if you're a team manager, the new teacher at school, or a city council member, person-to-person relationships can be an incredibly useful outlet for your energy.

IN A MORE OPEN RELATIONSHIP SYSTEM, PEOPLE:

- Have more frequent contact.
- Have more authentic contact.
- Are open with their thinking about important issues.
- Understand how people tend to see the world.
- Show respect for differences in thinking.

IN A MORE CLOSED RELATIONSHIP SYSTEM, PEOPLE:

- Have less frequent contact.
- Have less substantive contact.
- Have less access to others' thoughts about important issues.
- Keep secrets from one another.
- Guess what other people are thinking.
- Show no respect for differences in thinking.

I know that there can be exceptions to these ideas. I'm not saying that you sit at the dinner table while someone is saying harmful things, or ask your QAnon cousin which celebrity he thinks is a lizard person. This is simply the idea that it's useful to have access to people and their thinking about certain challenges. So is being open with people about your thinking. This is true for any group that is working on a goal. Making decisions based on people's real thinking, rather than your best guess, helps a group more effectively reach their goals and manage tension. It can direct its energy toward solving real problems, not hypothetical relationship drama.

Sylvie was ready to have a person-to-person relationship with her grandmother. Her family had shifted into cutoff, but the system was beginning to open up. And she wanted to play a part in this. So one Sunday, at a Wendy's off the New Jersey Turnpike, she had lunch with Grandma Lynn for the first time since preschool. They started small, chatting about Arizona weather and Sylvie's job. Ready to shoot her shot, Sylvie brought up the hurt she'd experienced from the family cutoff and her desire to move forward in a different way. Her grandmother apologized, they hugged, and they promised to see each other again soon.

Problem solved, right? Not exactly. Sylvie was dismayed that her anxiety was still churning after their first meeting. They stayed in contact through texting, but Sylvie didn't feel motivated to call her grandmother or make plans for their next visit. *Is this what our relationship is going to be?* she wondered. *Polite chatting and pictures of the rattlesnakes in her backyard?*

MOVING PAST SMALL TALK

Sylvie kept up relatively superficial contact with her grandmother: a comment about weekend plans, reactions to snakes and lizards, a brief birthday call. Sylvie was curious to learn about her grandmother's life, but asking felt like an intrusion. And she might not like what she found. What if her grandmother thought Tucker Carlson raised some good points? What if she had cheated on Sylvie's grandfather? What if she wasn't that interesting of a person?

When clients feel stuck in superficial family relationships, I often encourage them to imagine they are catching up with a close friend over coffee. What joys, challenges, and interests are you telling them about? What questions are you asking them? How are you wondering about the world together? What might it look like to operate this way with family members? In other relationships?

We often never get to the good stuff because we stick with "safe questions" in social settings.

COMMON SAFE QUESTIONS:

- How are you doing?
- How's work?
- How was your weekend?
- What are you doing for [insert holiday]?

- Have you talked to [other person] lately?
- How is [other person] doing?

There is nothing wrong with these questions. They can be useful in building relationships. But they are questions that invite superficial responses. If you ask the barista at the coffee shop how they're doing, you'd be surprised if they began to describe an existential crisis. We know the routine questions and answers we're supposed to give, and we fall into this rhythm just as easily with those close to us. It takes effort to think of questions that engage a person's thinking and experiences.

SOME PERSON-TO-PERSON QUESTIONS:

- What have you been excited about lately?
- What do you wish other people knew about you?
- What's something that's been challenging for you lately?
- What do you think the family's (group's, organization's, etc.) challenges are?
- What's your version of a perfect day?
- What's been keeping you awake at night recently?
- When have you felt the freest in life?
- What would you love for the next decade of your life to look like?
- If you could be any fictional character for a day, who would you choose?
- If you could give a lecture on a weird topic without any preparation, what would it be?

Sylvie used safe questions in her contact with her grandmother. She knew so little about her grandmother's life. She was curious to know the good and bad in her marriage with Sylvie's grandfather. She wanted to know her hopes for the family as they reconnected, her hopes for her grandchildren, and her hopes for herself in her retirement years. All of these questions would be a gift to give her grandmother, and the information would be a gift to Sylvie.

Obviously these questions cannot be tackled over a single Baconator sandwich. But starting this kind of contact, called "emotional contact" in Bowen theory, is invaluable. Gathering family history gives us context to people's decisions and reactions. Learning about people's interests and challenges helps us feel connected and curious. When we learn about people's plans for the future, we don't have to guess what they want or expect from us. Emotional contact connects us to the real person, not the people we might imagine they are or fear they might be. It also helps us build a more solid self through our relationships with others.

STOP KEEPING SCORE IN YOUR RELATIONSHIPS

When people begin to operate more thoughtfully in their relationships, they often hit a roadblock: keeping score. People might not ask you as many questions as you ask them. They might not respond to every message, or only see you when you issue the invitation. A seemingly self-absorbed parent, an inconsiderate sibling, or a radio-silent friend are convenient excuses to reduce contact.

Anxiously focusing on how people communicate may be a sign of relationship orientation. We become angry or frustrated that others aren't functioning the way we are. This is the togetherness force pulling at your brain. *Do as I do! Be as considerate as I am, Christopher!*

YOU KEEP SCORE IN RELATIONSHIPS WHEN YOU:

- Refuse to contact family members who rarely contact you.
- Complain that someone never asks you about yourself.
- Refuse to visit family because they don't visit you.
- Deliberately stall your reply to a person who is slow to reply to you.
- Maintain distance because it's been too long since you've spoken.
- Become defensive when someone suddenly becomes interested in you.

This isn't a call to maintain every friendship until you die. Or the suggestion that you always have to host Thanksgiving dinner. It's simply the idea that not every relationship is about feeling equally supported. Which, I realize, sounds like an absolutely bonkers thing for a therapist to say. But it's useful to keep asking your dad to coffee if it teaches you how to be yourself around him. If you stay in contact with that super-anxious colleague, you get a chance to practice self-regulating your anxiety. Sometimes important relationships are opportunities to be a more responsible self.

Our culture loves to talk about "feeling heard" or "being seen" in our relationships. These are nice things, but they are responses we have no control over. Focusing too much on them can increase the anxiety.

WE OFTEN ASK OURSELVES:

- Do I feel heard?
- Do I feel seen?
- Do I feel understood?

BUT WE CAN ALSO ASK OURSELVES:

- How would I like to communicate my thinking?
- Did I represent my thoughts/feelings the way I wanted to?
- Am I creating opportunities to define myself to this person?

The popular wisdom these days is to cut everyone out of your life who isn't "building you up." But how far do you take this chainsaw mentality? And how much are other people really responsible for building you up? We don't work on differentiation by only associating with people who function, think, and communicate the way we do or want them to.

When you focus on being the kind of person you want to be, the other person might become more comfortable with more emotional contact. They might even begin to initiate it themselves. But what if they don't? What if your brother always mumbles one-word answers when you call him? What if your mother continues to ask the world's most unhelpful questions?

We all have fantasies about how we'd like relationships to be. But if the goal of bridging distance is to turn your family into supporting characters who are fascinated by your awesomeness, then you'll likely be disappointed. The more you are able to express your own maturity with family, or other groups in your life, the more you can enjoy relationships with imperfect people. People who push back at some of your decisions. People who struggle to make plans. People who want to talk to you about cryptocurrency.

I can think of many examples where ending a relationship is the absolute best course of action. Working on differentiation does *not* mean that you put up with abuse or anything that is harmful. But it might mean that you reconnect with that aunt who just fell off the radar. It may require you to speak up when a friend is inconsiderate instead of quietly sulking off. It might even mean reconciling with someone after a twenty-year feud.

How do you figure out whether ending contact is the right course of action? Bowen theory asks people to consider whether the choice is a thoughtful response to a challenge, or an outcome driven by emotional reactivity. It's not about the choice, but the intensity, the emotional reactivity behind the response. Often people who are quick to cut off will see history of the pattern in their family diagram. It was the button pushed as soon as the tension rises. What is the long-term cost for a family when multiple generations don't have access to one another? The cost when we're quick to drop friends at the first sign of tension? Often the result is that the remaining relationships will feel very stifling and intense.

Sometimes our anxiety is spot-on. We need to get the hell out of a situation or a relationship. And sometimes, it's useful to do the opposite of what anxiety would have you do. Often our anxiety wants us to stay very quiet in relationships, to maintain the superficial stability we achieved. It wants us to avoid bridging cutoff because there are too many unknowns. This is why our capacity to step outside the intensity of the system, to engage our best thinking, is so important. When we're paying attention, we begin to see which relationships can help us learn to be a little truer to ourselves. The relationships where hanging in there, without giving in or giving up, makes all the difference.

FINDING REAL CONNECTION

Sylvie had a lot of courage. She was fostering new friendships, and reengaging old ones, but the process was frustrating. New and old friends didn't always buy into her offers. She usually was the one to make plans or follow up. Rather than stewing in resentment over people's flakiness, Sylvie decided to keep at it. If she was the one in therapy thinking about relationship building, then it made sense that she would be the one issuing invitations and broaching deeper conversations. She would have to be the weirdo who asked unique questions.

So Sylvie started inviting her friends to hang out one-on-one. If someone suggested watching *The Office* for the millionth time, she insisted that she was more interested in hearing about them. She also tried to stop and give an honest answer when people asked how she was doing. She admitted to people that she had felt lonely since her move to DC, and she even discussed her feelings of awkwardness at social events.

Sylvie thought she was being more authentic, but the work generated a lot of anxiety. She lost a lot of sleep, overanalyzing conversations with friends as she lay in bed. In our meetings, we talked about how her brain was simply serving its evolutionary function. A keen ability to intuit the thoughts of others was a true gift when the stakes were high, like being kicked out of your ancient, ancestral campsite. But someone thinking she was slightly weird at a happy hour? Not the same threat. Sylvie tried to remind herself that her anxiety was a sign of progress, a marker that she was growing into unknown territory. She was moving toward herself, and letting people see it. Over time, it didn't feel so scary.

Meanwhile, the texting game wasn't going anywhere with Grandma Lynn. Sylvie was learning a lot about the fauna of the Southwest, but very little about her grandmother. Sylvie suggested they schedule a phone call once a week to catch up. Because emotional contact didn't come naturally with her grandmother, she made a list of conversation topics before the call. If her mind drew a blank, she used an AI chatbot to generate bad questions, which made her think of better ones. The conversation could go where they wanted, but at least she had some ideas to fill the uncomfortable silence.

Over time, Sylvie learned more about her grandmother's life. About the ups and downs of getting married when you're pregnant and nineteen years old. The challenges of a spouse's death when you've been together your entire adult life. The ways we all borrow a little self from our relationships. Sometimes they talked about superficial things, like baking tips or the weirdness of Arizona. Other times they drifted toward more serious topics, like whether Benson and Stabler would ever get together on *Law & Order: SVU*.

Sylvie had imagined that reconnecting with her grandmother would be like riding a bicycle after a long break—a little bumpy until her instincts kicked in. But what she learned is that there is little naturalness in relationship building, especially in a family that has dealt with anxiety through cutoff. Without tending, our relationships almost always shift into gossip about others or the safest topics. It takes a great deal of effort to relate to one another as individuals, and to maintain that level of connection. But when you keep at it, the rewards are great.

One reward for Sylvie was an invitation to her grandmother's eightieth birthday party. It was the first time the entire family had gathered in more than twenty years. There was plenty of awkwardness, but Sylvie had laid the foundation for a person-to-person relationship with her grandmother. Her aunts, uncles, and cousins were all next on the list. She was connecting the dots between her relationship challenges. She could see how being herself with her grandmother could help her be more vulnerable in friendships. Distance was always an option in tense moments, but it was no longer the only option. She was ready to share more of herself with others and see what happened. It would be awkward, and it would be wonderful.

EXERCISE 1: **Flavors of distance.** What are the ways you use distance in your relationships? If you need examples, take a look at the chart below. What are upcoming opportunities for you to rely less on distance to manage stress? How can you work on building person-to-person relationships?

Family	Work	Partner/ Spouse	Friendships
Duty visits with lots of people as buffers	Only communicating electronically	Only talking about kids	Gossiping about friends
Gossiping about other family members	Gossiping about colleagues	Only watching television together	Only reminiscing about the past
Living very far away	Operating in silos	Needing alcohol/drugs to connect	Only sharing internet memes
Focusing on what a good boy the dog is	Not bothering to learn names and roles	Not speaking up about boundaries	Only gathering in groups

EXERCISE 2: **Be the weirdo!** If you need an official challenge to be an engaging weirdo, here it is. Try it at happy hour or the next family gathering. Be the person who asks people, "What are you excited about

these days?" Try out the list of person-to-person questions, and see if they energize a relationship. Maybe you'll find someone who's passionate about saving monarch butterflies. Someone who is also worried about the Yellowstone supervolcano (don't look it up). You'll never find them if you're always asking people what they do for a living, Dave!

EXERCISE 3: **Abandon the scoreboard.** Think about the friends and family you've been quick to write off because they haven't reached out to you. How do you want to represent yourself as a friend or loved one? Perhaps the enjoyment of seeing them is worth the price of making plans. Maybe you can summon some emotional courage and ask them to plan the next meeting. How can you focus less on the numbers game and more on the benefits of being yourself in this relationship? When you do decide to let people slip away, how can you do this thoughtfully rather than anxiously?

CHAPTER NUGGETS

- Distance is another relationship pattern used to manage anxiety. We often distance in response to relationship pressure. We use emotional distance when we hide our thinking, beliefs, and true self from others.
- The most extreme form of distance is cutoff. Cutoff can lower the intensity in a relationship, but it does not resolve the amount of fusion in a relationship.
- Distancing prevents us from working on differentiation of self in our relationships.

- Chronic anxiety is the anxiety generated by relationship challenges. Chronic anxiety distorts how we perceive others and can make us more "allergic" to them.
- Developing person-to-person relationships is an important part of increasing one's own maturity.
- A person-to-person relationship is one where you are able to talk about your beliefs and experiences, avoid focusing on other people, and not rely on superficial topics.
- The more person-to-person relationships you have in a relationship system, the more flexibly the system can function.
- A person who is building stronger person-to-person relationships is not relying on safe, superficial questions. Instead, they are asking questions about a person's thinking and experiences, and they are sharing their own. This is called emotional contact.
- Emotional contact connects us to the real person—not the person we imagine they are.
- Focusing on how people communicate can be a sign of relationship orientation. Rather than keeping score in relationships, focus on who you want to be in them.
- The more you are able to express your own maturity in relationships, the less you'll have to distance to manage tension.

7

HOW WE END UP BLAMING OTHERS

"I've never loved anything the way I love you, and I've never fretted on anything more."

—Maarva Andor, *Andor*

LUCAS WAS A surprise baby, an unbelievable gift to a couple who'd assumed they'd never have a child. His parents, Dave and Cindy, had been worried about him since day one, when he landed in the NICU. Lucas had a brilliant, creative mind, but he approached the world with caution and struggled to make friends. For college he'd attended a prestigious art school, but he flew home often to cope with the stress. Lucas's life was full of stops and starts, lots of treatment for depression, anxiety, and self-harm. "If we can just get him through this crisis," his parents reassured themselves, "everything will be okay."

Now Lucas was twenty-eight. He lived alone and kept a part-time job at a local nonprofit, helping senior citizens make beautiful art. Lucas was financially dependent upon his parents who paid for his rent, his transportation, his takeout orders, and his art supplies. Newly retired, Dave spent much of his day over at Lucas's, helping with tasks that overwhelmed his son. The washing machine was broken. A picture needed hanging. He needed a ride to pick up his medication. Dave didn't mind running errands for his son at all hours of the day. Cindy, however, had other feelings.

Cindy was a surgeon with significant income, enough that they could afford to do all these things for Lucas without feeling any pinch. But Cindy was tired of watching her son max out her credit cards. It wasn't the money, it was the principle, she told Dave. A twenty-eight-year-old didn't need to order out for every meal. But Dave had little interest in rocking the boat. Lucas was doing well, so why take the risk? If he fell into a depressive episode, or threatened to harm himself, Dave, not Cindy, would be the one managing his care.

Cindy and her son had frequent arguments about money. In moments of anger, she would threaten to take Lucas off her credit card, limiting him to the monthly check she sent. Lucas would call Dave in a panic, accusing his mother of financial abuse. Dave was furious that Cindy hadn't consulted with him, and he secretly began to slip Lucas large amounts of cash. When Cindy found out, she insisted that she and her husband go to therapy.

As you read this story, let me ask you a question. Who's the problem? That might sound harsh, but when most people read a story, they search for someone to blame. Maybe you felt frustrated at Lucas for not meeting the societal definition of "launching." Maybe you were annoyed by Dave's struggle to say no to his son. Maybe you were angry at Cindy for her impulsive decisions and threats. A lot of your reaction may have to do with your age, your own family's story, or other norms and values.

Humans are narrative creatures. We make sense of the world through stories. And in most stories, there are heroes and villains. There are people to blame, and those who are blameless. We tell these stories in our families, and we tell them on a societal level. This is because blame can be an adaptive response to stress. But when we look at a human story strictly through the lens of blame, we miss the emotional process at work. We see people as individual actors, rather than parts of an emotional system that is struggling to attain stability through predictable patterns.

TRIANGLES AND THE FAMILY PROJECTION PROCESS

You've learned about three of these predictable, anxiety-managing patterns in the book so far: conflict, over- and underfunctioning, and distance. A fourth mechanism is what Bowen called a "triangle," or "emotional triangle." When two-person relationships become tense, we sometimes use a third person to stabilize them. This could look like focusing our blame or worry on a third person. Or pulling in a third person to complain or gossip about the other. Bowen considered the triangle to be the building block of relationship systems.

Look closely at your family or your workplace, and you'll see that triangles are activated to calm things down. You'll find them in the natural world as well. A female chimpanzee will move toward a more dominant male when she feels threatened by his subordinate. Wolves will pick on the omegas (stuck at the bottom of the social hierarchy), and it seems to provide some stability to the pack. Triangles are not good or bad. They are simply one way that an emotional system manages tension.

TRIANGLING CAN LOOK LIKE:

- Gossiping about a third person.
- Venting to a third person.
- Worrying about a third person.
- Blaming a third person.
- Using a third person as a messenger.
- Relying on a third person as a buffer.
- Playing mediator/peacemaker between two people.

Triangles are the way that the emotional challenges of one generation get transferred to the next generation. Two parents (or caregivers) may manage their anxiety through

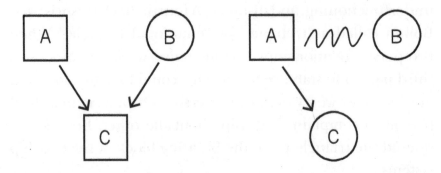

Figure 5. Triangles (left to right). In the first example, two people focus on a third to stabilize their relationship. In the second, a person (A) experiences conflict with another (B). They may pull another to complain or ask for advice on how to deal with the conflict.

an intense focus on the child. In Bowen theory, this is known as the "family projection process." Highly tuned in to the parents' distress, the child is likely to react in an anxious way, confirming the parents' worries. In other words, treat a child like you can't trust their decisions, and they may lose trust in them as well. Treat a child as if they need your encouragement to be motivated, and they probably won't function well without it. Over time, the child is shaped by the parents' worries, embodying them in their sensitivities and challenges.

I'm not saying that anxiously focusing on your kid causes their depression. This is the cause-and-effect thinking that leads to blame. But we do know that stress makes us more vulnerable to emotional, mental, physical, and relationship challenges. No one thrives under an anxious focus. It's much harder to be responsible for yourself. The more a child is involved in the patterns to keep things calm, the more relationship oriented they may become. The less differentiated they may be. They may be even more sensitive to others' reactions than their parents are. Without realizing it, they can become quite powerful, directing the family's actions to revolve around them.

Who are the kids who are more likely to catch the focus of the parents? This depends on a number of variables. Oldest or youngest children may be in a more vulnerable position. A child born during a stressful time in the family may be in the hot spot. The only boy or the only girl may draw the anxious attention of their parents, or perhaps it's a child who has a number of medical challenges early in life. What's important to remember is that the family projection process is an emotional pattern in the system, not

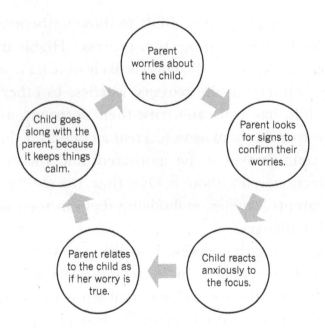

Figure 6. The cycle of child focus.

the parents' conscious plan to screw someone over. Children do things that invite our intense focus, and vice versa. There are times in the family when anxiety is high, and times when it isn't.

An only child who arrived on the scene prematurely, Lucas was a primary target for the family projection process. Both Dave and Cindy had distant relationships with their own families, so there weren't many people available to triangle in, to take on the stress generated in their little nuclear family. Therefore, worrying about Lucas had become one pattern, one lever to pull to resolve the tension in Dave and Cindy's relationship. This focus on their son kept them steady for decades. But the constant activation of this relationship pattern came at a great cost to Lucas.

SEEING THE WHOLE ELEPHANT

Dave, Cindy, and Lucas were a very anxious triangle. Lucas grew more panicked about his financial situation, and he placed more demands on Dave, who amped up his overfunctioning. Cindy grew resentful of the time Dave spent with Lucas, and she began to distance from her son. She canceled one of her credit cards, and they had a huge fight. Lucas called her a few choice words, and Cindy cut off all contact with him. Now the only parent on call, Dave felt even more obligated to comply with Lucas's requests. His own functioning took a nose dive. He couldn't fall asleep at night, and he started experiencing migraines.

This is what happens when typical relationship patterns can no longer successfully manage the level of anxiety in a system—people start to develop symptoms. And it's much easier to focus on symptom relief in therapy than thinking about the patterns that create a vulnerability to symptoms. In other words, Dave could work on relieving his migraines (as he should), but he would also benefit from thinking about the patterns that created this vulnerability to physical, mental, and emotional symptoms.

At first, Dave was more interested in blaming than seeing patterns. He spent a lot of time bemoaning the cutoff between Lucas and Cindy. "Things cannot get better until they start to talk," he said. Conversely, Cindy saw Dave as the solution to her problems. "If he could just learn to say no to Lucas, we wouldn't be in this mess." Lucas saw his parents as the ones needing to change. They simply needed to do what he asked, and stop jerking him back and forth with their financial support.

Each person in this triangle was blaming another for their misery. And because there was truth in everyone's viewpoint, it was easy to stay stuck in blame mode. The reactivity was so high, doing anything different felt terrifying. It felt like admitting you were the problem.

There's an old parable from India about a group of blind men who come across an elephant. The first puts his hands on the elephant's side and announces he's found a wall. The second feels the elephant's tusks and declares the object to be a spear. The third grabs the elephant's tail, saying it's a snake. The debate continues as the men touch other parts of the elephant. The men continue to quarrel as the elephant ambles away.

Systems thinking is an attempt to see the whole elephant. Because when anxiety goes up, we cling to our part of the elephant, our view from our corner of the relationship system. But seeing the group as an emotional unit, trying its best to keep things calm, well, that opens things up. We can operate with more flexibility and agency when we don't have to label one person as the solution to the drama.

WE MISS THE "WHOLE ELEPHANT" WHEN WE:

- Insist that one person needs to do the changing.
- Try to drag others toward maturity rather than expressing our own.
- Blame one parent rather than considering how both operate.
- Focus on others' responsibilities and not your own.
- Think about the current generation and not previous ones.
- Focus on personality flaws rather than patterns in relationships.

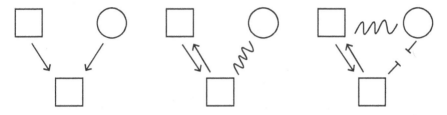

Figure 7. Shifts in a triangle (left to right). This triangle is relatively stable for a long time, with a focus on the child. As anxiety increases, the child invites more attention from the parents. Dad increases attention on the child, while Mom reacts by taking a hard, hasty stance which leads to conflict. Eventually, Mom and child cut off contact, while Dad continues his overinvolvement with the child. Both Mom and Dad demand that the other parent change their position.

- Focus on diagnosing rather than seeing behavior as adaptive.
- Ignore how anxiety influences our actions.

Dave, Cindy, and Lucas were clinging to different ends of the elephant. Dave observed his wife bolting in the face of a great challenge in the family. He saw his son struggling to be independent despite this cutoff. Cindy saw her husband, overwhelmed by the demands of their son, unable to determine what Lucas really needed. Lucas saw two adults who struggled to be consistent or thoughtful in their relationship with him.

Everyone had their eyes on different sides of the triangle. Conveniently, the side in which they played no part. Dave was focused on how Cindy needed to relate to Lucas. Cindy was focused on how Dave needed to relate to Lucas. And Lucas was convinced his parents were colluding against him. None of them were thinking about the larger, extended family. A family where distance and cutoff between the generations perhaps had helped intensify the relating inside this anxious threesome. Who would be the first to start seeing the whole triangle at work? To focus on their own part in the pattern, rather than just the immaturity of others? To think about these challenges in the context of the broader family system?

THE ANXIETY OF THE MOMENT

In times of stress, we are driven by the feelings of the moment. We are more focused on getting *comfortable* than getting it right. Every person in an anxious triangle is trying to get in a more comfortable position. If a friend is mad at you, it's comfortable to go to another friend and vent. If a relationship feels awkward, gossiping about a third person might help you bond. If your marriage is unsteady, focusing on "fixing" a child can unite you. Seeing a person's actions as their best attempt to calm themselves down, rather than a strategy to piss you off, can change how you think about the dilemma.

Is there a way of being in relationship with others that is less focused on comfort? Where no one has to pay the price? This is the idea behind differentiation of self. A person who is working on their own emotional maturity is willing to not do what they'd normally do to get comfortable. To relieve what Bowen called the "anxiety of the moment." But each person's path toward differentiation looks different from another's. So we cannot do this work to change others. We do it to change ourselves.

Dave, Cindy, and Lucas were seeking relief at the expense of the others. Though each rationalized their reaction as a logical response, in truth they were simply trying to get comfortable in the triangle. Cutoff had kept Cindy comfortable, while overfunctioning and underfunctioning had steadied Dave and Lucas to some degree.

Dave's comfort zone	Cindy's comfort zone	Lucas's comfort zone
Rushing to help	Cutting off contact	Letting others overfunction
Complaining about not being appreciated	Complaining about being neglected	Calling for help when distressed
Taking over when others are struggling	Threatening to punish	Accusing others of conspiring against him
Lecturing people on why they're wrong	Lecturing people on why they're wrong	Lecturing people on why they're wrong

How does a person begin to move out of these comfort zones? To start, you have to generate some operating instructions that are true to your best thinking. Dave realized that he'd never bothered to develop his thinking about how to treat Lucas like a responsible adult. Instead, he'd focused on questions like, "How do I keep Lucas from spiraling into depression? How do I make my wife less angry?" No wonder he was quick to accommodate them both. He was drowning in the anxiety of the moment.

Initially, Cindy had seen her swift actions as a principled stance against Lucas's financial demands. By considering the whole system, she saw how her actions were an attempt to get comfortable. Cutoff wasn't a viable solution for the long term. She wasn't interested in a life without Lucas, nor was she interested in parenting by random threat.

Dave and Cindy were stuck in what is often called a "soft/hard parenting split." And they were beginning to see the reciprocity, the interconnectedness, of their reactions. Cindy's "tough" responses and eventual cutoff had invited Dave's softer approach, full of overfunctioning and accommodating. And Dave's overinvolvement with Lucas had given Cindy more opportunity to bolt. Neither had a strong person-to-person relationship with their son, their reactions influenced heavily by Lucas's distress and the other parent's choices. One parent getting a little more thoughtful about their part might allow the other to do the same. My hope for Dave and Cindy was that they could both get out of each other's way as they figured out how to relate to their son with their best thinking.

WHAT THE HECK DO PEOPLE NEED?

In chapter 6, you learned that chronic anxiety distorts our perception of others. People tend to seem needier, more annoying, or more aloof than they really are. We're more likely to personalize people's behaviors. And we tend to think people need less or more from us than they really do. This is the paradox of chronic anxiety in a family—we focus on one another so much that we cease to know one another at all.

No relationship demonstrates this better than the one between parent and child. When you're distressed, or your child is distressed, reality quickly flies out the window.

Children do things to invite our anxious focus and our overfunctioning. And we do things that invite their under-functioning. So often our reactions have more to do with relieving our own anxiety than helping a child. Teasing apart a child's real needs from our anxious perception is no simple thing, but it can be useful for a parent to sit down and think about the difference.

Perceived Needs	Real Needs
My child needs me to get her to stop screaming.	My child needs me to be present and calm when she is distressed.
My spouse needs me to intervene when they're frustrated with our kid.	My spouse needs me to not undermine their relationship with our kid.
My friend needs me to give her advice when she's flailing.	My friend needs me to manage my own reactivity as I'm listening.
My organization needs me to go along with their unrealistic demands.	My organization needs me to be thoughtful about what I can and can't do.
My father needs me to talk to his doctor for him.	My father needs someone who makes space for him to think about his health.

Assessing real needs can be a useful exercise for any relationship. So often we let anxiety trick us into feeling overwhelmed by the nonexistent needs of others. Maybe you assume your friend wants an hour-long phone call when a short check-in will do. Maybe you think your boss needs constant updates about a project when in reality they trust you to follow through. Sometimes people will place demands on us that we're unwilling to meet, and what the relationship needs is our honesty, or our capacity to set and hold a boundary. But if we don't make an attempt to separate our best thinking from the anxiety, we end up simply giving in to others' demands, distancing, or overfunctioning for them.

Dave began to think about what Lucas needed from him. Sometimes there were real, tangible needs, like help moving furniture or navigating the health care system. But Lucas also needed a dad who took a deep breath or two before he picked up the phone. Maybe even a dad who let some calls go to voicemail, or said, "Let me think about that," before he said yes or no to a request. What he didn't need was a dad who feared Lucas was going to explode or harm himself every time he said no. A dad who treated him like he couldn't navigate life's challenges.

Cindy also thought about what Lucas needed from her. And what he needed was contact with a thoughtful mother who didn't make threats. He needed evidence that she wasn't going anywhere, even when she disagreed with him or set a boundary. That if she did say no, she wasn't saying it out of spite or exhaustion. Perhaps he also needed a mother who was working on her relationships in her extended family. Relationships with people who could also relate to Lucas in a less anxious way than his parents.

It's no coincidence that a more differentiated response from one parent would look a little different from the other.

But could they stay out of each other's way as they thought about how to relate to their son?

THE DISCOMFORT OF DIFFERENTIATION

Working on their own person-to-person relationship, Dave agreed to accompany Cindy to a work conference. They left town with great trepidation because they knew what to expect. The closer they appeared, the more Lucas would feel like he was on the outside. Based on past evidence, they predicted he would call with some sort of pseudo-emergency. There was a high chance he would ask his dad to come home. To prepare for this possibility, Dave thought about what constituted an emergency and what didn't, so the anxiety of the moment wouldn't convince him otherwise.

The first night of the trip, Dave got a string of urgent texts and voicemails from Lucas. His garbage disposal was leaking. He implored his dad to come home, arguing that his anxiety couldn't handle the stress of water damage in his apartment. Dave felt the urge to ignore Lucas or quickly solve the problem. Instead he called his son and said, "You've put a bucket under the sink. I'm willing to take a look at it on Monday when I stop by. If it gets worse, you'll have to figure out an alternate solution." Problem solved, right?

Lucas did not like this response. He argued how these setbacks were keeping him from independence. He claimed his dad was patronizing him, and if he did spend a lot of money on a plumber, Dave would yell at him. Dave replied, "I trust you to make smart decisions." Then, instead of hanging up angrily, Dave hung in there. He started to tell Lucas about the trip. And Lucas promptly hung up on him.

Dave's work on his own maturity didn't make Lucas magically respond in a certain way. But differentiation does not require any particular response from others. In fact, a move toward differentiation usually invites initial pushback from the system, which communicates, "Change back!" But Dave had momentarily hopped off the Ferris wheel. He knew he couldn't make decisions that were only about keeping Lucas calm. He owed his son, and himself, more than that.

After the trip, Cindy began her own efforts toward differentiation. She reached out to Lucas, but she also started to work on developing stronger person-to-person relationships with her own family. Lucas didn't take her calls at first, but he started to visit when his grandparents came to town. Initially annoyed by Lucas's attempts to ignore her, Cindy made herself stay in the room and participate in conversations with everyone. She sent Lucas an email, apologizing for cutting off contact and creating such whiplash with her financial decisions. "You deserve a mother who is more thoughtful about her actions," she told him. "I'm going to try and be that person." Slowly but surely, Dave and Cindy were bringing a little more solid self to their relationship with their son, and with each other. They would always be in the triangle, but they were able to operate more as individuals inside of it.

Tension gets managed in a family one way or another. Sometimes it's anxiously monitoring a child with challenges. Sometimes the parents are so fixated on each other's flaws that the kids manage to escape the focus. Or people only feel steady when they have a real or metaphorical ocean between them. The cards get dealt one way or another, and we must decide what we'll do with them. We can blame, or we can zoom out. We can continue with the way things are, getting comfortable at the cost of others. Or we can be more responsible for ourselves, freeing everyone from the patterns that keep us stuck.

EXERCISE 1: **Who caught the anxious focus?** Who in your family caught the most anxious focus from others? Was it one of your siblings? A parent who had health problems? What about your workplace? Has anyone been a convenient scapegoat or villain for people to blame for problems in the system? Think about how you have participated in anxious focus in different groups. Is there a way to relate to these people that is less about worry or blame? Write down your ideas.

EXERCISE 2: **Look for the triangles.** What are the relationship triangles that have been challenging in your life over the years? The one with your parents? Have you been caught between a parent and grandparent, or felt on the outside when a parent or child started dating someone? Have you mediated arguments between your partner and your child, two friends, or colleagues who just couldn't get along? What would it look like to operate more thoughtfully in each of these triangles, relating to each person on a person-to-person level?

EXERCISE 3: **Embracing the anxiety of the moment.** What do you do to relieve the anxiety of the moment? Are you more likely to accommodate, avoid, or act out? Are you overfunctioning for others, or acting less capable than you are? Are you getting on your soapbox and giving a speech about what others should do? We all have our ways of getting comfortable. Are there ways of responding to challenges that are less automatic for you and a little closer to who you'd like to be as a person? Describe what you might look like when you respond in a way that is truer to yourself.

CHAPTER NUGGETS

- Because humans are narrative creatures, we are quick to label people as heroes and villains in real life. Blame is one way we look at a story, but using a systems lens can help you see the reciprocal patterns at work.

- People will often pull in or focus on a third person to manage tension in a two-person relationship. This is known as a triangle. The higher the anxiety in the system, the more triangles may be used to manage the tension.

- Four relationship patterns used to manage anxiety in a system include conflict, over- and underfunctioning, distance, and triangles.

- Parents will sometimes transfer their emotional challenges to a child by focusing on them. This begins a process, known as the family projection process, in which the child is shaped by the sensitivities of the parents.

- Some children are more likely to be involved in the family projection process than others, depending on a number of variables.

- Each person in a triangle is trying to get in a comfortable position, but this comes at a cost to others.

- When relationship patterns can no longer manage the level of stress in the system, people may begin to develop symptoms.

- When we label one person as the one who needs to change, we miss seeing the whole system at work.
- It is useful to know how you relieve the anxiety of the moment in your relationships. By recognizing these behaviors, you create opportunities to act on your best thinking instead.
- Chronic anxiety distorts our perception of others. Working on differentiation of self requires you to distinguish between what someone really needs and what you anxiously perceive them to need.
- Working on differentiation of self may look different for each person in a family.

PART II

HOW WE FIND
OURSELVES

The first half of this book was about the relationship patterns that keep us from being ourselves. As much as we love to be special, humans are predictable creatures. We're predictable because we belong to larger emotional systems, like the family, that are doing their best to keep things calm and stable. These systems will vary in how rigidly they operate—how much they permit people to function as individuals. Add more anxiety to the system, and it's very difficult to operate outside the patterns.

To live a life that is truer to you, it's useful to understand the ways you lose self—the capacity to think and act as an individual—in a relationship system. Maybe you like to keep your relationships light and superficial, using distance to avoid any tension. Maybe you end up overfunctioning, directing everyone so you feel steady. Perhaps you've been quick to triangle other people into conflict, unsure of your own thinking. By studying the ways we get comfortable in our relationships, we begin to see opportunities to operate at a higher level of differentiation, to make decisions based on our own reasoning. Because there are more ways to be a person in the world than our original emotional programming.

This next section of the book is about moving past patterns and building something new. We'll explore what it looks like to function as more of an individual in your goals, challenges, and relationships. You'll meet people who learned to focus less on societal measures of success. People who stepped back from overfunctioning so others could surprise them. People who became more responsible for themselves without an army of experts. I'll share stories of people who added substance to their superficial relationships, and people who found the courage to define their beliefs to others.

There is no magical recipe for maturity in any of these stories. My aim is to give you a different way of thinking about human behavior, a systems lens provided by Bowen theory. A person who is curious about their part in relationship patterns is a person who can respond a little more thoughtfully to life's challenges. What that response will be is up to you. I hope that these chapters inspire you to live outside the reactions that simply keep things comfortable. To switch off your factory settings and keep evolving.

8

ENDING THE CHASE FOR APPROVAL AND ATTENTION

"If there's one thing I can't stand, it's snobbery and one-upmanship. People trying to pretend they're superior. Makes it so much harder for those of us who really are."

—Hyacinth Bucket, *Keeping Up Appearances*

JULIAN WAS A go-getter. At least that was what his teachers said when he graduated high school a year early by taking classes at the local community college. For undergrad, he hopped from classes to internships to part-time jobs, stockpiling course credits, money, and the attention of his professors. At night he dreamed about retiring at age forty, traveling around the world and learning new languages. And about how impressed people would be. Why take your sweet time with goals when you can attack the hell out of them?

Unfortunately for Julian, the ego boosts from his accomplishments evaporated faster than he could earn them. Like most of us, his spurts of productivity were slowed by bumps in the road and burnout. Midway through college, he studied abroad in Brazil. A month into the semester he broke his leg playing soccer, and the program shipped him back home to Utah. Stuck on his mother's couch, he racked up online course credits, finishing college before his twenty-first birthday. But he was burnt out, and still grieving his failed trip abroad. He had no energy left to make any career moves. Julian spent the next three years working at his aunt's catering company where he served tiny sandwiches and met another go-getter named Lauren. Eager to achieve power couple status, they psyched each other up, dumped their uniforms, and drove their belongings across the country to DC. Julian was going to graduate school for public health, Lauren was going to start a business, and they would never look back.

All went according to plan, until the spring of 2020. Suddenly, Julian and his girlfriend were trapped in their tiny studio apartment, sitting in front of their screens all day. They only had each other, so can you guess what happened? The fusion kicked in, and they both became experts at what the other was doing wrong.

Graduation was fast approaching for Julian, and Lauren began to lecture him about studying harder and finding a job. In turn, he criticized her excessive marijuana use and strange sleep habits. One night they had a big fight, and Lauren took the next flight out of Reagan back to Utah. Weeks passed as Julian furiously studied his unanswered texts and Lauren's cryptic Instagram posts. He was ready to toss her stuff in the nearest dumpster, but he also suspected he might take her back the second she came home. Trying to function without a companion felt impossible.

Julian felt his productivity begin to flatline. Would he find a job by the time he graduated? Or would he fall back into a slump, eventually calling his aunt to get his old job back? What happened to the go-getter who had wowed his professors?

WHERE DO YOU RANK?

Washington, DC, can be a tough place to feel successful. Everywhere you turn, you're confronted with aggressively motivated people. They have the audacity to jog in ninety-five-degree weather, or wear a suit on the Metro when you're in yesterday's sweatpants. Some are only interested in what you can do for them. Others want you to make impressed noises when they talk about their recent meeting at the White House. Only very close friends or their therapist can see what's lurking underneath an impressive résumé.

Though this particular flavor of professional zeal may be unique to DC, the obsession with status isn't. Social mammals, including humans, evolved to care about hierarchy for good reasons. Male chimpanzees will compete for a chance to groom their higher-ranking peers. A lower-ranking elephant will pay respects to his superior by placing his vulnerable trunk in the other's mouth. Humans aren't much different. If a higher-status person like a boss, a religious leader, or a popular kid asks how we're doing, this makes us feel good. We know that we rank in the group and will not be forgotten.

Cultural evolution, our ability to learn and adopt traits by nongenetic means, makes us excellent at copying and pasting the attributes of high-ranking people. Researchers have observed that people will mimic the speech patterns of people who socially outrank them. Small children will notice which adults get the most attention and instinctively copy their actions and choices. This is no surprise to me, a person who collected the wardrobe of my favorite TV character in my twenties. Copying our "superiors" is a convenient answer to the constant question "What should I care about in life?" Also, "What will keep me in the group's favor?"

Growing up, Julian had tried his hardest to outrank his peers. He loved being the kid who had graduated a year early, the one flying to Brazil when his peers were sleeping through chemistry class. But then he was a guy taking classes in his mom's living room. So he turned into the high-energy college student with laser focus—until he became the townie who might never make it out. Now graduation was approaching, and Julian noticed he wasn't landing a job as fast as his classmates. He could feel himself slipping down the imaginary leaderboard, and he worried he'd slip into deep despair.

Self-comparison is unavoidable when you're a social creature. We need to know where we rank so we don't become an easy target for the group. But if you've been paying attention so far, you know that humans also have the capacity to go against the group. The capacity to compare our actions with our internal compass. *How do I measure up to the group?* can be a useful question. *Do my actions align with my best thinking?* is even better. Julian tried to take his anxious thoughts about others and turn them into questions that explored his own beliefs.

EXTERNAL COMPARISON: Am I finding a job as quickly as everyone else?

INTERNAL COMPASS: What does it look like to be responsible for job hunting every week?

EXTERNAL COMPARISON: Am I working as hard as my girlfriend was?
INTERNAL COMPASS: What does a responsible, reasonable amount of work look like to me?

EXTERNAL COMPARISON: Do people look impressed when I tell them about my accomplishments?
INTERNAL COMPASS: When do my efforts align with my values? When do they not?

EXTERNAL COMPARISON: Is my mom worried about me?
INTERNAL COMPASS: How do I think I'm doing?

The goal isn't to eliminate one's tendency to self-compare. Please, show some respect for your social nature. But you can find opportunities to put down the ruler and pick up the compass. Moments when you can stand outside the noise and ask some good questions. We all have thoughts that reflect our true north more than others. Thoughts that are more solid self than pseudo-self.

COMPLIMENTS TASTE LIKE CAKE

Which would you rather have: a piece of chocolate cake, or an email full of praise from someone you admire? Many would choose the latter. When someone compliments us, our brain's reward system responds much as it would to a forkful of cake or a fistful of cash. It releases delicious dopamine, keeping us motivated and focused. We need incentives to stay connected to the group, and our brains have come up with some pretty tasty adaptations. The short-term bursts of fuzzy feelings we get from attention or approval keep us in line with the group and its rules.

The trouble with praise, however, is that we never know exactly when we're going to get it. Some of the time your boss will compliment your work, and other times they'll be too busy. A teacher might distribute your work as an example to the class, and the next day they'll choose someone else's. You would think this might discourage us from chasing the high, but the opposite occurs. More dopamine is released in anticipation of a reward if there is a 50 percent chance of getting it, compared to a 100 percent chance. Translation: it feels good to gamble for people's attention. Like regulars at a casino, we pull the lever and hope for a head pat.

Experts at mentalizing, we also constantly consider how others perceive us. Even the slightest chance of being watched makes us behave better. Put a mirror in front of someone (or a set of cartoon eyes on the wall), and they are less likely to misbehave and more likely to be generous. While other animals can recognize themselves in a mirror, the self-control triggered by our own reflection is unique to humans. Even when we are alone, we carry the watchful eyes of the group with us. What we label as our own self-consciousness is actually a conversation between our urges and how other people might react to them. No one is truly the monarch of their own mind.

Julian could waste a lot of energy trying to force himself to stop liking attention and approval. Or he could accept that cake is tasty, and try to think differently about the problem. Finding a job in Julian's chosen field, public health, was no simple thing. If it was something he wanted, he had to be able to tolerate short-term disappointments while he worked on his long-term goals. He would have to live with less attention and approval, without his standard rocket fuel, while he pursued these goals.

All problems are chances to build a more solid self. But the more anxiety they generate, the more likely we are to choose the fastest, most socially approved solutions. Caught up in the daily cake chasing, we easily lose the larger plot of our lives. Julian tried to see the opportunities for maturity that lurked behind the crisis of the week.

IMMEDIATE PROBLEM: I need a job that makes me look good.
OPPORTUNITY FOR MATURITY: I need to learn how to define myself in more ways than my job title.

IMMEDIATE PROBLEM: I have to network with people, and I'd rather jump into a volcano.
OPPORTUNITY FOR MATURITY: I need to learn to be more comfortable being in relationships where I'm the one receiving help.

IMMEDIATE PROBLEM: Why the bleep won't my girlfriend text me back?
OPPORTUNITY FOR MATURITY: I need to think about how to respond when others act immaturely.

Julian faced real challenges. He had to pay the bills, build connections, and figure out his love life. He could smoke out these problems as quickly as possible, or use them to help fill the gaps in his maturity. He could work on differentiation, or he could stay stuck in relationship orientation, guided by thoughts like *I'm not good enough for my girlfriend,* or *People are secretly annoyed when I ask for help.* He could be a mind reader, or a mind knower.

KEEPING UP APPEARANCES

As a child, I loved watching the British sitcom *Keeping Up Appearances* with my parents. In every episode, middle-class social climber Hyacinth Bucket ("Pronounced *bouquet!*" she'd insist) tries to impress her peers with her snobbish demeanor and famous candlelit suppers. Mortified by her background, she desperately attempts (and fails) to hide her working-class relatives, who pop up at the most inconvenient times.

We spend so much of our energy trying to look put together, or mimicking "higher-ranked" peers. We try to teach the people we love how not to embarrass us, or we hide them from sight. Like Hyacinth, in our efforts to please we become caricatures of ourselves.

When you were growing up, how much did your family focus on keeping up appearances?

KEEPING UP APPEARANCES COULD LOOK LIKE:

- Not letting people visit unless the house is spotless.
- Talking more about children who are more "successful."
- Only posting "perfect" pictures on social media.
- Purchasing things you can't really afford.
- Shaming family members for embarrassing you in public.

- Not introducing family members/friends to people who might dislike them.
- Not letting people dress, speak, act like themselves.

We think about the family system not to blame them, but to take the temperature of the togetherness force. How much were people guided by others' reactions and not self? I think of my own mother panic-cleaning when someone announced they were coming over. The times she gave me the signature mommy death stare when I misbehaved at the grocery store. This communicated a message loud and clear—"We cannot let people know that we are messy."

Julian's addiction to approval didn't exist in a vacuum. The gaps in his own maturity spoke to the functioning of his family system. And in Julian's family, the focus on appearances ran deep. He'd been raised by his mother and grandmother, the latter a woman who treated life like a zero-sum game. When he visited his grandmother, she would update him on the successes (or lack thereof) of his cousins and childhood friends. She was quick to comment on who had moved into a bigger house, who had a drinking problem, and who had gained weight. He had purposely kept his distance after college when he'd worked for his aunt, imagining what his grandmother was saying (or not saying) to others about him. When he was accepted into graduate school, she'd paraded him around town like a prized poodle.

Julian's mom had been much more supportive during his ups and downs, but he knew she was nervous about this next transition. His older sister had a physical disability, and his mother would sometimes direct the same level of anxious focus on him. Succeeding had been his way of relating to his mother who'd finished law school with two small kids and was now a judge beloved by his hometown. Julian could feel everyone in his family (except his sister, bless her) holding their breath those final weeks before graduation. Would he make them proud, or would he be someone they spoke about in vague terms?

Julian was motivated to please his family, but this outward focus felt paralyzing when he wasn't doing well. These borrowed beliefs about life and success didn't reflect his best thinking. He didn't care whether his friends were considered accomplished or not. He usually was turned off by people who were trying their hardest to impress him. So why did he make himself the exception to these rules? He needed to shed some pseudo-self and figure out his next steps.

SOLUTIONS FOR GROWN-UPS

As discussed in chapter 7, so many of our decisions are focused on relieving the anxiety of the moment. Making decisions that are true to you requires you to tolerate some distress. In his book *Bowen Theory's Secrets*, Dr. Michael Kerr calls these decisions "grown-up solutions." I love this phrase, because asking yourself, *What is the grown-up solution here?* can jump-start some good thinking. It can also highlight all our reactions that haven't been all that mature.

One way to work toward grown-up solutions is to determine whether you're giving your challenges anxious attention or thoughtful attention. Anxious attention is focused on anxiety relief. It leads to fast, borrowed, and socially approved solutions and the predictable patterns in the relationship system. Thoughtful attention is trying to get at what the real challenges are, what the real needs are. It's an attempt to function a little outside of the emotional process. It acknowledges that distress is par for the course as you find the best way forward. Bowen and Kerr called this the "anxiety of progression."

ANXIOUS ATTENTION CAN LOOK LIKE:

- Trying to manage or fix others.
- Letting others manage or fix you.
- Treating your imagination as reality.
- Abandoning your thinking for quick or popular solutions.
- Focusing on what you "should" do.

THOUGHTFUL ATTENTION CAN LOOK LIKE:

- Attempting to manage anxiety before responding.
- Taking time to gather facts.
- Defining your thinking before acting.
- Sitting with the discomfort of a more differentiated response.
- Sitting with the discomfort that problem-solving takes time.

Julian was at a crossroads. He could fly home to see Lauren and do whatever she wanted to get her back. He could sign up for fifty networking events and try to impress the heck out of everyone. Or he could do some good thinking. How could he handle this transition without careening toward burnout? How could he manage his fears of being alone, or being stuck in a dead-end job forever, while slowly proving to himself that he was capable?

Julian had spent most of his days suppressing these fears only to find them clawing through his brain every night. So he began to schedule twenty minutes every day to give them some thoughtful attention. When he greeted his anxiety like a friend over coffee, a few grown-up solutions began to reveal themselves. To start, he had to work on relationship building in his chosen career field. But Julian was allergic to networking, forever hating relationships that felt trans-actional. His initial response had been to distance, to stop building these relationships altogether. A grown-up solution might be to build relationships on his own terms, outside of boring happy hours. He'd also have to put some work in to be able to ask people specific questions, rather than the anxious "Can I pick your brain?" request.

Another grown-up solution was to communicate his thinking to his girlfriend rather than trying to wait her out or win her back. She wouldn't pick up the phone, so Julian sent her a long email with his thoughts. He emphasized that he did care about her, but he was interested in a relationship with someone who defined her thinking rather than mak-ing him guess. He gave her a month to grab her things or take over the lease on their apartment.

Julian also took a deep breath and looked at the reality of his finances. He set a date when he'd have to start look-ing for hourly work to stay afloat. He also stopped avoiding phone calls from family. He didn't need to communicate all of his worries and plans to his mother and grandmother, but regular updates about his life were an important part of staying connected. Those relationships could be more than just a place to report successes. Julian suspected that if they could sense his own maturity in handling this transition, they would likely calm down.

Julian could see that being a grown-up and being "impressive" are not always the same thing. He was taking a crisis point and turning it into an opportunity to do something different from the most successful-looking thing. He was teaching himself that he could hop off the hamster wheel, the unending chase for evaporating ego boosts. This was more of a gift to his future self than landing any job or nailing any interview. His own maturity, his willingness to be thoughtful, kind, and patient—these were his superpowers. Powers that had nothing to do with anyone else's reaction.

EXERCISE 1: **Copying and pasting your way through life.** When have you tried to mimic those who socially outranked you? Did you try to dress like your more popular peers in high school? Have you parroted the speech of an impressive boss or mentor? Organized your apartment like your favorite influencer? Perhaps no thought or decision can ever be 100 percent original, but some of our choices have more self in them than others. Where in life would you like to be less of a copy-and-paster? What might this look like?

EXERCISE 2: **Cake chasing.** Compliments have their purpose. But how do you know when too much of your day is spent chasing after those chocolate cake feelings you get from praise or attention? When have you betrayed your best thinking for doing what gets the most approval? List three examples where you've gotten caught up in approval hunting.

EXERCISE 3: **Solutions for grown-ups.** Think of a few challenges you're facing right now. If you tried calming things down as quickly as possible, how would you react? If you were trying to implement grown-up solutions to these problems, how might your responses look different? Try making space in your weekly schedule for thinking about grown-up solutions to life's challenges.

CHAPTER NUGGETS

- Because humans depend on social groups to survive, we are experts at evaluating where we rank in a group. Humans will mimic the behaviors of their higher-ranking peers from a young age.
- Cultural evolution, our ability to learn and adopt traits by nongenetic means, makes us excellent at this mimicry.
- Humans use self-comparison as a form of fast evaluation. But we also have the capacity to be guided by an internal compass—our own thinking and beliefs.
- Approval and attention are reinforced by the brain's reward system. These social rewards are a powerful adaptation that keeps us cooperating with the group. Even when we are alone, we are considering what others would say about our actions.
- We spend a great deal of energy "keeping up appearances" to earn or retain social rewards. The degree of energy you invest in these efforts is influenced by your family system's relationship orientation.
- Giving your challenges thoughtful attention, rather than an anxious attention, provides an opportunity for grown-up solutions. These solutions come with some amount of discomfort because they are less focused on relieving anxiety or maintaining social status.

9

LEARNING TO LET PEOPLE SURPRISE US

"Who am I if I can't carry it all?"

—Luisa Madrigal, *Encanto*

NAIMA'S HUSBAND, ERIC, looked at his phone too much. He left his clothes on the floor, and when she asked him to clean them up, he piled them in a chair. The lawn needed mowing, the bathroom sink was clogged, and their two boys wouldn't stop sitting on each other's head. But Eric didn't notice any of these things. He was too busy grumbling at something on the internet.

Naima and Eric had met on the job, two twentysomething reporters sent to cover city council meetings. Naima loved Eric's spontaneity and sense of adventure, his willingness to exit the highway and visit any and every tourist trap. He adored her tenacity, chasing after a story when people tried to shut her out. They perfectly balanced each other, until the kids came along.

Soon after their youngest turned four, Eric lost his media job. While he searched for a new one, every semi-decent habit he had seemed to evaporate. Watching his confidence plummet, Naima was quick to swoop in and take over. Eventually Eric found a job, but his capabilities at home never rebounded. Their initial compatibility now felt like a broken seesaw.

At first, Naima fumed quietly, reading articles on women's emotional labor to feel vindicated. And then she not-so-quietly complained, demanding that Eric be a more responsible human. He would step up for a few days, emptying the dishwasher or doing the laundry without being asked. But when Naima gave him pointers on his efforts, he'd sulk and slip back into his underfunctioning. And the cycle would begin again.

With their tenth anniversary approaching, Naima couldn't see a way forward in their marriage if they kept spinning in a cycle of distance, criticism, and accommodation. She fantasized about leaving Eric, but she also had dreams where he begged for forgiveness and magically did better. She sensed that the right path for them was somewhere in the middle.

THE DANGER OF CHANGING SELF TO CHANGE OTHERS

Ever the journalist, Naima did her homework. She read a lot about Bowen theory, and she was interested in interrupting her relationship pattern with Eric. She knew she was overfunctioning in her marriage. She was willing to do anything, *anything* to get Eric to step up more at home. And right there was the problem. She believed that if she stopped overfunctioning, if she let the grass grow high enough, or stopped buying paper towels, her husband would do something. Weeks later, she was still wiping her hands on her pants and the front yard was a nature preserve. Why hadn't her strategy worked?

Humans are experts at self-delusion. Often we think we are working on ourselves when we are not. We're simply trying to manipulate others by tinkering with our own behavior. The goals we claim for ourselves are secretly the goals we have for others.

PEOPLE HOPE THAT IF THEY CHANGE THEIR BEHAVIOR, THEN:

- Other people will become more responsible.
- Other people will calm down.
- Their child will behave.
- Their friends will agree with them.
- Others will realize how wrong they are.
- An estranged family member will talk to them again.
- Those random people will think they're cool.

This is one of the pitfalls when people first learn about Bowen theory. The theory does assert that a relationship system can gain flexibility when one person is working on their own maturity. So when a person makes a series of seemingly mature moves, they expect others to adjust accordingly, to level up as well. But they find that their toddler is still screaming, their mother is still calling twelve times a day, and their husband has put an empty ice cube tray back in the freezer. Seriously, what kind of person does that?

I do not know how to make people change. Especially people I've never even met. But I do know that differentiation of self is not a video game. You cannot push a series of buttons and get the desired result. Humans are much wilier than that. They can sense when they're trying to be manipulated, and they also have this thing called free will, which is just the absolute worst.

Naima's strategy might have changed, but the level of fusion in her marriage had not. Her laser focus on Eric was just as strong, if not more so. She watched him like a scientist, waiting for her brilliant experiment to work. Whether she was doing nothing for Eric, or doing everything for him, the *level of intensity* was the same. At least when she was overfunctioning, she didn't have to worry about getting Lyme disease from walking to the mailbox.

Changes in our relationships do not come about through aggressive, anxious reposturing. They happen when we begin to think differently about the problem. Getting the yard mowed was a problem, but it wasn't *the* problem. Naima's problem was the one we face in any relationship—how do you respond to the immaturity that inevitably shows up in others? Do you respond with your own flavor of immaturity, or something a little more thoughtful?

A person who is working on differentiation is asking questions that center their own responses, not questions that focus on "fixing" the other's immaturity. This is the shift from relationship orientation to working on yourself.

RELATIONSHIP ORIENTATION: How do I get my husband to be more responsible?

SELF-FOCUS: How do I respond with maturity to my spouse's immaturity?

RELATIONSHIP ORIENTATION: How do I get my friends to hang out more?

SELF-FOCUS: What do I think is a respectful way to reach out to my friends?

RELATIONSHIP ORIENTATION: How do I get my kid to behave in public?
SELF-FOCUS: How do I want to manage myself when my kid throws a fit?

RELATIONSHIP ORIENTATION: How can I convince my girlfriend to go to therapy?
SELF-FOCUS: Can I get clearer about what I can and cannot do for her?

Naima realized she'd been responding to Eric's irresponsibility with her own flavor of immaturity. Passive aggressively forgetting to buy paper towels wasn't more effective than aggressively sticking Post-it Note reminders on Eric's steering wheel. Anxiously watching Eric give the kids a bath wasn't more helpful than taking over and doing it herself. Both reflected the high level of fusion in the relationship.

Naima tried to think about what it *really* looked like to step back in her overfunctioning. It looked a little different from being an anxious supervisor or giving up. It looked more like being a patient observer of the process. When Naima began to take a few deep breaths, lower her heart rate, and simply pay attention, she noticed a few new things. She noticed how much more patient her husband was when the boys were helping with a chore. That he didn't fret so much when one was a little behind his peers with a developmental milestone. He didn't get bored playing dinosaur ninjas for the thousandth time. Sure, he also had his challenges. If a kid refused to brush their teeth or clean their room, he quickly became distressed and called for her. But Naima was beginning to see the reality of his functioning, both the assets and the deficits. She was thinking more clearly about how to respond when Eric's actions invited her overfunctioning.

LOVE LANGUAGE OR ANXIETY LANGUAGE?

People love to poke fun at Gary Chapman's very popular book *The Five Love Languages*. I'm sure he's laughing all the way to the bank. The book explores the idea that many relationship problems emerge from a disconnect in how we express love. In other words, don't keep buying your partner flowers if they want to hear some nice words.

I'm sure there's a fair amount of truth to this idea. But when clients start talking to me about love languages, I tell them I'm interested in hearing about their anxiety language. What do they do to keep things calm in a relationship? How does their partner expect them to keep things calm? Because often there's no disconnect at all. Both people are operating in a reciprocal pattern, a borrowing and lending of self that works at relatively low levels of stress. A perfectly imperfect match.

RECIPROCAL PATTERNS IN RELATIONSHIPS:

- One person does too much, and the other lets them.
- One person avoids, and the other anxiously pursues them.
- Both people are trying to change each other.
- Both people worry about a child.

A person who is thinking in terms of love languages may ask themselves, *Are my needs being met?* This is one of the slipperiest questions you can ask in a relationship, simply because it's a great way to dial up the anxiety. Trying to get your partner to express love in a particular way can be fusion in disguise. And it often has the opposite effect. I'm not saying you never ask for a hug or a romantic weekend. But an anxious focus on the other can stifle the intimacy and creativity in a relationship. It promotes togetherness at the expense of individuality.

Rather than asking if your needs are being met, try asking yourself, *What am I doing to meet my needs in this relationship?* Here are some examples.

GETTING YOUR NEEDS MET: Why don't you ever hug me?
MEETING YOUR OWN NEEDS: Could I give you a hug? That would make me feel much better.

GETTING YOUR NEEDS MET: Why don't we ever go on romantic trips?
MEETING YOUR OWN NEEDS: I'd like to plan a romantic trip for us. I'm willing to book the travel if you'd be willing to plan the activities.

GETTING YOUR NEEDS MET: Why didn't you text me? Don't you think about me at all?
MEETING YOUR OWN NEEDS: I'm going to send you emails while you're away because I think it would be fun. I'd love to hear what's going on with you as well.

When we're evaluating others, we can't forget another important variable—the level of chronic anxiety in the system. Have you ever noticed that a person's quirks will bother you less on a calm day? The higher the level of anxiety, the more we tend to feel neglected. The more annoyed, the less tolerant we become. An unenthusiastic kiss or a pair of pants on the floor is going to feel like a five-alarm fire. Try asking yourself, *Have these behaviors become a real problem? Or am I increasing the focus on them to manage stress?* Sometimes it's a real problem that needs to be discussed. Boundaries need to be set. Responsibilities need to be more evenly distributed. But other times, it will be the latter. You'll need to work on managing your own anxiety in a different way.

This is what I suspect happened with Naima and Eric. The stressors of parenthood, job transitions, and financial strain were a pressure cooker, where they both developed an expertise in the other's imperfections. Naima carefully studied Eric's habits and shortcomings. When she didn't feel good enough as a mother, she often tried to teach Eric how to relate to the boys. She was worried about her own screen time, so she carefully studied his phone habits. When the house felt too chaotic, she focused on his lawn maintenance. Everywhere she looked, alarm bells went off. *Is this a person who I can count on?* she wondered.

Look, Eric was no angel. He certainly dropped the ball in ways that invited Naima's focus. And he was deeply allergic to Naima's efforts to change him. If he sensed her potential disapproval, his capabilities shut down. Her anger was a convenient excuse for his own immaturity. If she was just going to criticize him, why try?

DIFFERENTIATION ISN'T SIMPLY
DOING THE OPPOSITE

When two people are stuck in relationship orientation, it's usually a sign that at least one of them needs to step back and zoom out. So often we can see in the previous generations what we cannot see in our own. Naima's best thinking didn't come from watching her own marriage. It emerged when she observed her parents' marriage. She watched how her father was content to do everything for her mother. Naima would occasionally scold her mother, telling her she needed to step up and help out around the house. "Leave your mother alone," her father would say. "She's fine." Naima realized her parents had settled into a comfortable over- and underfunctioning dynamic, one that wasn't her responsibility to interrupt.

When Naima thought about Eric's family, she also saw the patterns at work. Eric had grown up in a family where the men received great care and attention, where they looked to women to direct them. Eric's father was diagnosed with multiple sclerosis at a young age, and his mother and older sister had focused on caring for him. They had never expected Eric or his brother to participate in this care. No wonder he and Naima were such a perfectly imperfect match.

The last thing Naima wanted was to repeat the patterns of the previous generations. But ironically, her quest to do the opposite hadn't worked either. It's common for people to shift into reverse when it comes to their family's functioning. But what they often accomplish is simply creating a different flavor of immaturity. People with distant parents may put too much anxious focus on their children. People with dogmatic families may struggle to define any guiding principles for life. People who grow up in chaotic families may rule their own with an iron fist. These are reactions to the previous generations, rather than an attempts to define oneself.

When Naima dreamed about her marriage, she imagined she'd have an equal partnership where responsibilities were split fifty-fifty. But trying to anxiously force this division had made for a more contentious marriage than her parents' more relaxed eighty-twenty.

Naima didn't want to give in, overfunctioning for Eric for the next fifty years. But she also knew that the opposite approach, demanding Eric function as she functioned, was not differentiation. She had made the mistake of defining an equal partnership as a sameness in functioning. So how could they have a more equal marriage that also permitted them to be more of themselves? She sensed she needed to be more realistic about what their lives would look like if Eric became more responsible as an individual, not her twin or her dutiful assistant. There would be costs to her decision to step back, but these were much more tolerable than the cost of always taking over for her husband.

TEMPORARY COSTS OF STEPPING BACK FROM OVERFUNCTIONING

- The kids might have a weird lunch packed for school.
- Our lawn might not look great for a while.
- We may have a "clothes chair" in the house.
- My son might be upset that the night routine is a little different.

LONG-TERM COSTS OF NOT STEPPING BACK
FROM OVERFUNCTIONING

- My husband never learns how to plan for the day.
- I'll continue to feel exhausted and burned out.
- We'll keep having arguments about responsibilities.
- My husband will struggle to stay calm when my son is upset.

Looking at these two lists, you can see how the long-term costs usually outweigh short-term ones. A person can know this but still find it difficult to operationalize this wisdom. It's difficult to let colleagues run slower meetings than you would. It's hard to let somebody make a mess in the kitchen when you like to clean up as you cook. But sometimes we have to let people do things differently, less efficiently, or even more creatively if we want the relationship to be more flexible. If we want to preserve our own sanity.

Family relationships are full of these paradoxes. Children need structure and routine, but they also benefit when one parent doesn't do everything exactly the same way. It's good to make sure trash gets taken out on Tuesdays, and it's also nice to be able to manage your anxiety when it piles up a little. We need the skills to have conversations with our partners about their behavior, and we also need the capacity to stay in our damn lane. No one can tell you which situation calls for which response. This is why differentiation of self is not a list of five easy steps. "No-self" problems call for solutions that come from "self," not the convenient advice of others.

Perhaps Naima could have a more equal marriage. But she'd have to accept that Eric's fifty wouldn't look exactly like her fifty. Each of them could learn to be responsible in ways that looked a bit different.

BECOMING LESS ALLERGIC TO YOUR PARTNER

People can't surprise you unless you step back. But they also can't surprise you unless you stay connected to them. And connection is hard when fusion is high. The more we try to turn people into projects, the more we'll begin to see them as boring or irritating. At the beginning of a relationship, we are often the freest to be ourselves and let others be themselves. We have more energy to be genuinely interested in each other. Once you've been together for a while, the lines have blurred. You might assume there's nothing left to learn about someone. You're also more sensitive to their stress level, which can make you allergic to their problems.

This is why more "closeness" isn't necessarily the solution to spicing up a relationship, romantic or platonic. In fact, too much attention can be what's making the relationship taste so bland. Chronic anxiety is a major conversation killer. When you assume you have nothing left to learn about a person, curiosity evaporates. Treating someone like a separate individual, rather than one half of the relationship blob, is likely to make them more interesting.

Togetherness	Individuality
Needing your partner to parent a certain way.	Talking about your individual challenges as parents.
Only talking about things you're both interested in.	Talking about what's interesting to you. Focusing less on whether you're boring the other person.
Needing to know everything about your partner's day.	Creating space to share the highs and lows of the day.
Feeling responsible for fixing their problems.	Listening to their challenges without overfunctioning for them.

Naima could certainly relate. She was a journalist for goodness' sake. Engaging people and finding the interesting angle was her job. But when Eric started talking about local politics or his job stress, she found herself zoning out and nodding like a zombie. Sensing Naima's frustration, Eric showed little interest in her challenges. He was quick to dart out of the room when she started venting. How had they become so allergic to each other?

Naima realized that she'd felt over-responsible for Eric's work challenges, or at least for the anxiety they generated in him. No wonder she'd zoned out. She also didn't want to hear his opinions on local politics because she disagreed with them. She was allergic to his eagerness to prove her wrong, so she disengaged completely. She needed to find a third way through these challenges—to connect to Eric without giving in and overfunctioning, or giving up and distancing. She had to look for opportunities to stay in the room and talk, without having to play debate team.

Naima watched for an opening. One day, when Eric was ranting about the city council, she touched his shoulder and said, "Let me ask you a question. If you were on the council, what's something you'd try to accomplish in the first year?" After Eric's initial shock (had his wife been body-snatched?), he seemed to slow down and think. To her surprise, Naima realized that she was interested in hearing his answer. She also found she was interested in coming up with her own answer to the question. They'd both had a glimpse of what it looked like to operate outside of the regular push and pull of the togetherness. They were thinking, and relating, as individuals.

YOUR HOMEWORK IS YOURSELF

We've explored the benefits of *stepping back* to let people surprise you, and *stepping up* to stay connected to them. When anxiety is high in a relationship, it's also useful to *step out* to pursue our own goals. Our relationships benefit when we operate with a little more solid self inside the relationship, and a little more solid self outside of the relationship. Outside the relationship, we work on becoming a person who has goals and interests.

DIFFERENTIATION CAN LOOK LIKE:

- Stepping back to let people be responsible for themselves.

- Stepping up by staying connected to people.
- Stepping out to pursue what's important to you.

It's kind of a chicken-and-egg situation. Does being less relationship oriented make it easier to accomplish individual goals? Yes. Does working on individual goals help you be less relationship oriented? Also yes. I'm not saying that if you learn to play the French horn, your wife will become a better listener. Just that individual pursuits are sometimes a missing ingredient in an anxious system. Did you have a parent who pursued an interest when you were a kid? Or were they anxiously focused on you or someone else? Proximity to someone pursuing their interests can be a powerful thing.

Stepping Back (don't overfunction)	Stepping Up (stay connected)	Stepping Out (function like an individual)
Creating opportunities for people to show you they're capable.	Staying connected, even when you feel bored or anxious.	Pursuing your own goals and interests.
Letting people be responsible in their own way.	Sharing your thinking and creating opportunities for them to share theirs.	Not needing others to have the same goals and interests as you.
Managing your own anxiety while people function for themselves.	Thinking for yourself despite relationship pressure to think a certain way.	Working on yourself in other relationships.

For a mother of two young kids, a hobby felt like a pipe dream. But Naima did some good thinking about how to build up her sense of self when things at home were tense. She could redirect some of the energy spent analyzing Eric's habits and apply it toward herself. She started swimming with a friend in the neighborhood, and she signed up for an American Sign Language class at the library. Rather than resenting Eric's trips with his friends, she planned one with her friends. She was surprised to find that Eric encouraged her to do this. He was beginning to feel more confident in his solo time with the kids.

Naima began to notice that when she gave herself her own homework, both inside and outside the relationship, she was a little less focused on Eric's clothes chair, or how long he brushed the kids' teeth. She also kept working on her maturity in other relationships. By relating to her parents, her kids, and even her colleagues with more individuality, her marriage would only benefit.

If you're wondering whether Eric ever mowed the lawn, I honestly don't know. Naima never brought it up again, because she seemed to be less focused on evaluating his functioning. Growing up isn't about getting people to become more responsible. Nor is it learning to put up with people's bad behaviors. Sometimes people will surprise us, and other times they won't. But we give them the best chance when we relate to them as an individual.

EXERCISE 1: **Push a button, win a prize.** When have you tried to manipulate others into behaving better? Have you tried parenting techniques only to be frustrated when your kid still acts like a jerk? Have you cut down on gossiping at work only to find the rumor mill chugs right along? Have you tried to teach your partner to be more romantic only to have them fail spectacularly? Write down a few examples, and on a scale of one to ten, rate how anxiously focused you were on them. What might it look like to be self-focused rather than other-focused in these challenges?

EXERCISE 2: **What's your anxiety language?** What are the ways you've expected your partner to calm you down in a relationship? How have they expected you to calm them down? (If you're not in a romantic relationship, apply these questions to other relationships.) How would you like to be able to meet your own needs and manage your own distress? How can you relate to people in a way that allows them to do the same?

EXERCISE 3: **Grow your sense of self.** Have there been times in your life when focusing on your own goals has been useful for your relationships? What are small ways you can work on building up your sense of self, and put less pressure on a relationship to meet all your needs? What would make you feel confident and capable this week? This year?

CHAPTER NUGGETS

- Often we tinker with our behaviors in an attempt to change others. This does not change the level of fusion, or immature dependence, in a relationship.
- A person working on differentiation of self is focused on how they want to respond maturely to the other's immaturity.
- Rather than focusing on getting your needs met in a relationship, consider focusing on meeting your needs by how you represent yourself in the relationship.
- The higher the stress in an emotional system, the more we tend to feel neglected or annoyed by others.
- If you're bored by someone, it may be a sign that you aren't treating them as an individual. By treating them as an extension of yourself, you may become overinvolved in their challenges, and oversensitive to their emotional reactiveness.
- Differentiation can look like *stepping back* to let people be responsible for themselves, *stepping up* to stay connected, and *stepping out* to pursue individual goals.
- A person who is building a sense of self outside the relationship can operate more flexibly within the relationship.

10

BECOMING MORE
RESPONSIBLE FOR
OURSELVES

"I pretty much just do whatever Oprah tells me to."
—Liz Lemon, *30 Rock*

CRISTINA COULD READ a room like nobody's business. She was a thirty-something executive assistant, solving problems and smoothing over relationships for her very-much-a-big-deal boss, Linda. All of the complainers, criers, and crises were sent to Cristina, an expert at placating them. Linda asked Cristina to sit in on important board meetings where she secretly made notes about who scowled at her boss. Then they'd brainstorm for hours late into the evening, strategizing on how to keep everyone happy. When they weren't talking about work, Cristina would complain to Linda about her love life, her temptation to reach out to an ex she had blocked multiple times. Her boss was quick to dole out relationship advice and career advice while Cristina took notes.

Cristina had a habit of overinvolving people in her journey toward self-improvement. She had enlisted an army of professionals, gurus, and friends to help her grow. She had a nutritionist, a trainer, and even a personal astrologer. She would FaceTime friends to get tarot card readings. Her earbuds constantly blasted podcasts with dating coaches and financial advisors. Answers from others had a calming effect. They stilled her mind for a few hours, until the self-doubt would creep back in.

Cristina saw her life as a quest to correct her father's mistakes. Her mother had died when she was twelve, and her father never recovered. The oldest in the family, she was expected to fill in the gaps, caring for her younger siblings and managing her dad's moods. There were a million things she wished her father had done for her in return. He had never taught her how to believe in herself. He should have gotten her tested for learning disabilities. He didn't teach Cristina how to set boundaries in relationships, or how to make healthy choices for her body. He should have sent everyone, including himself, to therapy. And now her bank account was eating the cost of his under-involvement.

Cristina was great at taking directions, but terrible at directing herself. She excelled at being Linda's eyes and ears, but she struggled to pay attention to her own challenges. Without an expensive layer of professional accountability, her functioning seemed to plummet. She would order takeout when the fridge was full of food, or stay up until 2 A.M. scrolling through social media. When she felt bored, she'd unblock her ex Michael and start texting him, creating some drama just to feel excited about something. The next day she'd schedule a therapy appointment, trying to reel herself back toward better choices.

Cristina wanted to fly with a lighter crew, not an army

of experts eager to advise her. She wanted to trust her own thinking. To untangle herself from this weird symbiosis with her boss, and get past blaming her dad. But was it worth it to disrupt the relative stability she'd achieved? She wasn't sure.

READING THE ROOM IS OUR SUPERPOWER

The human brain is built for many tasks, but the most important is our ability to navigate drama. You may laugh, but it's true! Put a rhesus monkey into a bigger social group, and its prefrontal cortex will expand. Differences in the volume of the human prefrontal cortex can also predict the size of a human's social group.

Outlasting our less social Neanderthal cousins, we owe our species' success to our love for gathering in big groups. We're built to comprehend stories that involve many people and their relationships. We're skilled at guessing what others think about us, but we're also masters at determining where people stand with one another. Or whether they would get along if they met. This is why people love to analyze every eye roll in the British royal family. Why they spend hours planning their seating chart for a wedding. You know exactly why Aunt Marie would piss off your college roommate's girlfriend. This skill is known as "transitive inference," and only the smartest of social animals have it.

Think about a television show you love, one you've seen multiple times. You can probably describe every relationship between characters to a surprising degree. You might even be able to predict how these characters would respond to one another in a hypothetical scenario. Our social brains allow avid fans to write fan fiction that is astonishingly true to character. If a person can do this with fictional characters, consider how much more we know about the relationships between colleagues or family members? It's not hard to guess what scenarios would cause tension.

TRANSITIVE INFERENCE HELPS US:

- Avoid conflict.
- Defuse tension.
- Promote reconciliation.
- Seek allies.
- Be more effective leaders.
- Connect people to one another.
- Compete for social rank.

Despite the benefits, thinking about other people's relationships can eat a lot of our energy. The more you're tuned in to drama, the more you may struggle with productivity. Maybe you're an expert matchmaker, but flail in your own dating life. If you're the peacemaker in the family, you might find it difficult to talk about yourself. Knowledge of others does not translate automatically into knowledge of self.

Cristina's boss Linda expected her to quickly read others' intentions and disapproval, to map out the interpersonal landmines at work. Cristina was more than prepared, as she'd spent decades soothing squabbles between her dad and siblings. And her friends sought her out when they got a cryptic text from a date. It was both gratifying and exhausting to be treated with such deference. Meanwhile, Cristina's emails were piling up. She struggled to set boundaries in her own romantic relationships. And she found herself regressing to her teenage self with her family.

I'm skeptical that a person can turn off their tendency to monitor the relationships of others. It's too hardwired into us. People can, however, play around with the amount of energy we use to direct others. You can decide *how* you get information, and what you do with it. And you can redirect energy toward working on yourself.

If you spend a lot of time worrying about other people's relationships, it can be useful to ask yourself, *How am I getting my data?* Acquiring data through mind reading, gossip, and triangles may be an indicator that the anxiety is very high at work or in the family. And when stress is high, the boundaries between your responsibilities and others' responsibilities tend to blur.

OBSERVABLE DATA:

- The interpersonal challenges people talk about.
- Observations from group interactions, emails, etc.
- Observations of emotional patterns (triangling, distancing, etc.).
- Your own experiences with people.
- The factual history of the group or organization.
- The level of anxiety at the moment.

ANXIOUS DATA:

- Mind-reading everyone's thoughts/feelings.
- Seeking out gossip to get information.
- Speculating about people's relationships for fun.
- Getting information through triangles.
- Imagining how people might be upset with you.

When Cristina's brain was gathering anxious data, it felt like a club that never closed. Without any bouncers, the imagined reactions of coworkers, friends, and family crowded out her own thoughts. Perhaps it was time to let the health department shut the place down.

Eager to dial down her focus on others, Cristina tried changing a few behaviors at work. She stopped asking people in the hallway, "How are you doing?" like she was on an Easter egg hunt for interpersonal problems. Instead, she made people schedule a meeting with her where she asked good questions. If she found herself in a triangle with someone talking about another person's feelings, she didn't chase after them. She simply said, "They are welcome to come to me if they want to talk." She also tried to get clearer with herself about what was in her purview and what was an HR problem or a Linda problem. She started to ask people, "What do you think you're going to do?" rather than anxiously offering solutions. People were a little surprised at first, but Cristina began to learn that people can generate their own thinking.

Cristina also tried to report less anxious data to Linda. Rather than saying, "These are the people who might be upset with you," she began to say, "Here are the challenges as this person sees them." It was fascinating to see how switching from talking about people's feelings to people's thinking helped lower the intensity at work. Cristina was beginning to free up some energy that she could apply to her own pursuits.

MATURE AND IMMATURE DEPENDENCE ON OTHERS

When people first learn about differentiation of self, they often misinterpret it as an isolated endeavor. As if one has to retreat from all attachments to others, singularly driven by a purpose or principle. But differentiation is not about being Batman. I mean, have you looked at Batman's family diagram? Differentiation happens in relationships. We increase our level of maturity when we develop more mature connections to others. Refusing all help when you are sick is no more differentiated than letting someone wipe your nose. Doing all the work in a group project is no more differentiated than letting the overachievers run the show.

Immaturity takes on different flavors depending on how the system functions. My own immaturity is the mirror image of Cristina's. Ever the only child, I love to dream up a project and then do all the work myself. I struggle to let people add their own thinking and creativity to the mix for fear that it will slow us down. At first glance, this doesn't seem like dependence, but it is. My mood and functioning *depend* on others functioning exactly the way I do, or stepping back and letting me run the show. Get with the program, Denise, or get lost! So what would it look like to build a more mature dependence on others, one that respects people's capabilities and unique contributions? One that allows other people to share responsibility for the solutions? Let's just say I'm working on it.

Cristina had the opposite problem. She wanted everyone's input, all the time. So much that her own thinking never fully developed, or got lost in the mix. She'd spend hours talking with her ex Michael, asking him why he thought their relationship went wrong. She was quick to ask Linda, "How'd I do?" after she ran a meeting, without asking herself the same question. Cristina didn't add much of her own thinking in her meetings with her nutritionist or trainer. Therapy was difficult at times because she really wanted to know what I thought she should do. And I, the eager overfunctioner, really wanted to tell her.

AN IMMATURE DEPENDENCE
ON OTHERS LOOKS LIKE:

- Automatically asking people to do things you can do for yourself.
- Taking over and overfunctioning for others.
- Distancing to avoid tension or disagreement.
- Asking everyone's opinion without defining your own thinking.
- Needing everyone to think the same way about a challenge.
- Micromanaging everyone's efforts on a goal.

A MORE MATURE DEPENDENCE
ON OTHERS LOOKS LIKE:

- Working with others on shared goals.
- Connecting to talk about challenges and beliefs.
- Communicating real needs to others.
- Developing your own thinking and letting others do the same.
- Tolerance for differences in thinking about solutions.
- Respecting the capabilities and creativity of individuals.

Cristina found it hard to be curious about her challenges. Why let your mind wander when the certainty of others is ripe for the taking? Like Luis in chapter 5, Cristina was a content consumer, quick to quote the wisdom of others when she faced a challenge. By developing fawning relationships with hired professionals and parasocial relationships with famous experts, Cristina bought herself boosts in functioning. The trouble was that these were temporary and expensive boosts.

What do you do when you're like Cristina and you've spent years outsourcing your thinking to others? I don't think the solution is to pull a Kathleen and go it alone. Experts may have knowledge that can be useful to us. Groups have their own wisdom. But what does it look like to engage with professionals while bringing a little more self? To develop a mature dependence that is less about borrowing self, and more about defining yourself?

Here are some ways you could be more responsible for yourself in your work with experts (or expert content).

Responsible Work with Nutritionist	Responsible Work with Trainer	Responsible Consumption of Self-help Content	Responsible Work with Therapist
Bringing thoughtful questions to meetings.	Being honest about your challenges.	Choosing specific times to listen and learn.	Coming prepared to talk about various challenges.

Tracking useful information to report, and defining specific goals for yourself.	Practicing without "mat talk" to power through.	Journaling your takeaways/ critiques after listening.	Generating your own thinking about how to respond to challenges.
Determining the criteria for being able to fly solo.	Determining the criteria for being able to fly solo.	Making space to let your mind wander (without needing to listen).	Being honest when you want to take a break or discontinue the work.

This chart makes me think of the Alcoholics Anonymous saying "It works if you work it." Many people grow frustrated in their work with professionals because they expect the time to generate its own magic. And you might experience a boost in functioning if a therapist or coach is eager to tell you how to improve your life. But borrowing self from experts will not generate intrinsic motivation and curiosity, two necessary ingredients for long-term change. It's useful to come prepared for meetings and to develop your own definitions of progress.

There are many ways to be more responsibly involved in therapy. One approach is to take some time before a meeting to simply write down your thinking about your challenges and progress. What have you noticed? What have you been trying to do differently? How effective was this? It's less about having the solutions, and more about warming up the part of the brain that generates them. It prepares the mind to be a responsible part of the meeting so that you're less likely to invite the overfunctioning of your therapist or other professional. Because trust me, most helping professionals feel very comfortable overfunctioning.

True responsibility requires us to develop our own thinking. This thinking might be challenged and change over time, but it has to be ours. We give it a voice by using our own words. And we give it legs by taking those small, shaky steps toward greater maturity.

MOVING PAST PARENTAL BLAME

When you're fixated on others' immaturity, it can be very difficult to work on becoming a more responsible person. And when we're frustrated with our own functioning, it's easy to blame those who raised us. These are the people who taught us how to be (or not be) responsible. And most of our parents (or grandparents, caregivers, etc.) failed at this in some absolutely spectacular way. Maybe they never modeled how to manage money, how to disagree without screaming, or how to handle setbacks or failure. As someone who never had a bite of salad until my twenties, I get it.

Your brain evolved to create compelling narratives, to make sense of the world and those around you. Somewhere in this process, it learned to interpret negative outcomes as intentional, and positive outcomes as unintentional. Let's say your mother took you to the park every Friday when you were a kid. And you happened to meet your best friend there. You're more likely to see this event as a coincidence than the result of your mother's efforts. But if your mother took you to the playground and you fell off the monkey bars and broke your arm, you are more likely to blame her for being neglectful. When assessing negative consequences, the parts of your brain that process emotion (namely the amygdala, which helps you react in a crisis) become more activated. This natural, emotional bias makes it much harder to be objective when you think about people's behaviors. We are much more likely to blame them.

Blame is a stabilizing force in the emotional system. It can reflect an immature dependence on others, the idea that they must do better in order for you to do better. Bowen had a phrase for this dependence—"unresolved emotional attachment." Think of it as the immature dependence on others that is created in our childhood and carried with us into adulthood. It could look like always needing someone to reassure you, or always needing someone to boss around. Whether you have a relationship with a parent or not, this invisible dependence is still present, influencing all our relationships.

We resolve this immature dependence by working on differentiation of self. By learning to develop both our independence *and* a more mature dependence on others. And if those who raised you are still alive and in your life, then those relationships may be the best place to do this work of moving past blame.

Blaming her father helped Cristina manage her anxiety about her current life. Blame, however, does not increase one's own maturity. What does it take for a person to move past this intense level of blaming? Some people rely on a moral or spiritual belief in forgiveness to nudge them forward. But what many call forgiveness, you could also call a shift in perspective. Such a shift occurs when you can move from individual cause-and-effect thinking to multigenerational systems thinking. Yes, that means busting out the family diagram. Or interviewing older family members, or digging into the organization's archives. Whatever it takes to see the history of the system.

Cristina's paternal grandfather was the successful owner of a furniture store, a Romanian immigrant who'd built a great family legacy. Though he was the oldest sibling, her own father wasn't chosen to run the business. He'd had some medical challenges in his childhood, and the family had always treated him, and viewed him, as less capable. No one bothered to teach him how to manage money because they could always bail him out. Being told what to do was a comfortable position for him—so he found a wife, an oldest daughter who had filled that role until she died. Burdened with his own immature dependence on others, Cristina's father struggled to advocate for himself and his children.

Now Cristina was up to bat. Would the emotional process drag her along, keeping her over-responsible for others and under-responsible for herself? Keeping her stuck in blame? Or would she be able to move to a different beat, no longer personifying people's expectations of her? It would be a challenge to zoom out and stay curious when blaming her father was a convenient button to push.

Here are some examples of the shift in thinking that occurs when people move from blame to a broader, systems focus.

BLAMING FOCUS: Why can't my dad be more responsible?

SYSTEMS FOCUS: How did some siblings in the family end up more capable than others? To what extent was he treated like a responsible self in his family?

BLAMING FOCUS: Why does my mother have such a messy love life?

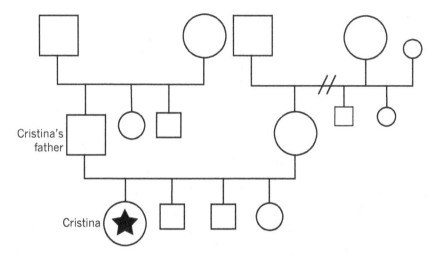

Figure 8. Cristina's family diagram. How does looking at the facts of the family, rather than focusing on one person, help us think differently about the past, present, and future?

SYSTEMS FOCUS: How did my mother use romantic relationships to resolve her own maturity gaps?

BLAMING FOCUS: Why didn't my grandmother get me the help I needed?

SYSTEMS FOCUS: What was the level of anxiety in the family during my childhood? How might this have made it difficult for her to see my real needs?

Moving past blame isn't an attempt to explain away people's agency. There are times when we do need to hold people accountable for wrongs. But accountability is an expression of self, a determination of how you will respond to the poor behavior of others. It is not an immature fixation on others to manage your own anxiety.

Systems thinking also helps us see the reciprocity in relationships across the generations. If a parent is less capable, were there people in their life who treated them like they were less capable? If they couldn't connect you to important resources, were there people always pointing them in the right direction? When you go back a generation, you may find it's a little harder to be mad at grandparents than parents. Because it's easier to see the whole picture. Thinking only about the current generation is a recipe for anxious blame. We're usually too affected by the chronic anxiety to see the bigger picture.

Cristina looked at her family diagram and thought about her father's role in his family. How had treating him as less than capable served to stabilize the system? Had he been caught up in the cycle of child focus, in the family projection process? Cristina saw how she was in a vulnerable spot as the oldest after her mother's death. It was no surprise that she became a person who was overcapable for others but not for self. She could even look to the future and predict how she might anxiously overcorrect in the next generation. If she had kids, they would be in no danger of neglect. If anything, she'd be too focused on them. They'd probably be assessed to no end, or sent to therapy the second they struggled with something.

How useful is this ability to predict! By thinking forward, we give ourselves opportunities to play around with our own responses. To see the million alternate universes that lie in front of us, rather than behind us. Suddenly, we have less need for a time machine, less desire to go back and yell at past generations to make good choices. Does it remain deeply unfair that the playing field isn't level, that we are born and raised by people with varying levels of emotional maturity? Of course. But we are not resigned to these fates. Our capacity to think and act as individuals says otherwise.

TAKING OFF YOUR TRAINING WHEELS

Bowen theory does not provide specific techniques for becoming more responsible. This is because Bowen himself saw techniques as just another flavor of relationship orientation, as an attempt to try to change other people. But the theory does describe a *process* by which a person can become a more responsible self. A path for taking off our training wheels, the patterns we use to feel steady. Patterns like distancing, over- and underfunctioning, or focusing on a child.

PROCESS OF BECOMING A MORE RESPONSIBLE SELF:

- Beginning to develop person-to-person relationships with family and other significant people.
- Learning to observe and change one's part in relationship patterns.
- Learning to manage one's own reactivity more responsibly.
- Developing one's own principles and beliefs.
- Learning to tolerate the distress that comes with living according to these principles and beliefs in relationships.

Bowen wrote, "That which is created in a relationship can be fixed in a relationship."

If the relationship system created the immature dependence, the relationship system is where you can learn to function more as an individual. Bowen theory places less emphasis on what happens in the therapy room. Differentiation is not a technique a therapist teaches; it happens in our person-to-person relationships where we hold on to whatever good thinking we have developed, where we practice being true to ourselves.

Is this approach the *right* way? I would say it's *one* way. Because surely there is more than one way to grow up in life. We all find ways to take off our training wheels and steady ourselves from within. People can decide for themselves how they move past resentment. How they become more responsible. How they pull back from being overinvolved with others. The answer isn't an answer. It is the ability to be curious about a good question. To hang in long enough to test an idea and see what's useful that comes out of it. To develop our own beliefs about how to be a person in the world.

Cristina thought a lot about the training wheels that steadied her. The beliefs she'd borrowed from experts. The blame she put on her father. Her overinvolvement with colleagues. How could she learn to trust her own ability to stay steady?

She started by developing a principle for getting help: anytime she made an appointment with a professional, she had to write down her own thinking before the meeting. Sometimes she found that she had good insights and questions to bring to the meeting. Other times she found that her thinking was sufficient, and she didn't need the stamp of approval from a professional. This allowed her work with experts to become more about growth and less about managing her anxiety. This was much more cost effective. Cristina was creating opportunities to try to wobble her way through problems. She was certain to crash into the bushes every now and then. But without her training wheels, she would move with more freedom.

Cristina also continued to untangle herself from Linda. She was less inclined to stay at the office late at night, and less likely to vent about her personal life. Linda was disappointed at first, but their time together became more productive. By operating more as a self at the office, she felt herself becoming more present and creative. Of course there were times when Cristina got sucked into the drama, but she tried hard to focus on her person-to-person relationships with people rather than the gossip that traveled through triangles. The drama would always be there, but she was beginning to operate a little more outside of its intensity.

Cristina also began to relate to her dad with less reactivity and with less blame. She had labeled him as the source of all her problems, but now she saw this relationship as a part of the solution. She called him often, trying to talk about her challenges with less bitterness. Rather than asking him "why" questions about her childhood (e.g. "Why couldn't you do this?") she focused on "who," "what," "where," "when," and "how" questions, learning what he was up against and how he had managed to make it through.

By having more person-to-person contact with her father, Cristina was teaching her brain to shift out of blame. There were different ways to relate to her dad, just as there were more hopeful ways of thinking about her challenges. Gradually, her future untethered itself from an anxious focus, an immature dependence, on her father. She was becoming a little more separate, but also a little more connected to him.

There were times when Cristina would forget all this thinking. She'd latch on to a new guru, fixate on the past, or send a "What's up?" text to her ex at 2 A.M. But she wasn't as hard on herself about it. When every moment is an opportunity to be a little more responsible, it's a little easier to stand up, brush yourself off, and try again.

EXERCISE 1: **Immature or mature dependence?** Think about the ways you've demonstrated an immature dependence on others in a group. Are you quick to take over, or quick to poll everyone for their opinion? Write down your ideas about how you can operate more as a self while respecting others in your family, at work, or in other groups.

EXERCISE 2: **Interrupting the blame game.** Make a list of three people you have blamed for the way you function today. How can you zoom out and think about the larger emotional system at work? What questions might be useful to ask? Write down a few ideas about what it might look like to be more responsible for yourself in adulthood.

EXERCISE 3: **Bring your responsible self to meetings.** Think about an important meeting with an "expert" you have coming up. Maybe it's with your doctor or therapist. Or a parent-teacher conference, or a performance review with your boss. What preparation will help you get the most out of this time? Are there regular questions you can ask yourself before every meeting? Write down your ideas.

CHAPTER NUGGETS

- The human brain is built to make interpretations about other people's relationships, a skill known as transitive inference.
- Thinking about relationship drama eats a lot of en-

ergy and attention, making it difficult to pursue our own goals. It can be helpful to distinguish between observable data and anxious data when thinking about relationship challenges.

- Working on differentiation of self involves becoming a more responsible self while developing a more mature dependence on others (rather than immature dependence).

- Rather than anxiously borrowing self from experts, we can bring our own good thinking to this work with professionals.

- Blame can be a sign of the unresolved emotional attachment, or immature dependence we have on others to function or regulate our mood.

- Taking a systems focus helps us move past blame and be more curious about past generations. It can also help us make predictions about the future.

- Bowen theory does not offer techniques for self-improvement, but it does describe a process by which a person can become more responsible for themselves.

11

BUILDING STRONGER RELATIONSHIPS

"I gained another pound today. But I think it's a pound of knowledge."

—Frankie Bergstein, *Grace and Frankie*

SHRIYA HATED CONFLICT. She would rather launch herself into the sun than say something that upset someone. Meanwhile, her four housemates could power a small town with their daily drama. Someone had accidentally let the cat loose. Somebody had stolen a watermelon LaCroix. Someone could not replace the toilet paper if their life depended on it. They had been friends since college, but such are the challenges of stuffing twentysomethings into a DC row house.

Shriya was anxious about integrating her new boyfriend, Cam, into the friend group. They were supportive, but she also knew they could dissect one another's love interests with chilling precision. So Shriya began to prep Cam, educating him about her friends' proclivities and topics he should avoid. If she could guide him safely through level one, her housemates, she would begin extensive preparation for level two: her family.

Shriya was the younger sister in a South Asian family. Her parents had emigrated to the US as young adults, working less than desirable jobs so their daughters could thrive. This dedication came with its own anxious focus. Shriya's mother was always very worried about everyone's health and appearance. She lectured Shriya on eating the right foods and dressing more professionally at work. Her father's mantra was "Respect your mother," and he said little more than that.

Too allergic to her mother, Shriya would triangle in her older sister, sending her as an envoy to discuss Shriya's grievances. "You need to stop being so hard on Shriya," her sister would scold until their mother would back off. Now Shriya feared how her mother would respond to her new boyfriend, with his penchant for greeting everyone with "Hey, man" and wearing graphic tees. Maybe she could just wait until it was time to send wedding invitations?

DE-CLUMPING OUR RELATIONSHIPS

We know that humans love a group. Whether it's joining a team or forming yet another committee at work, operating in fun little human pods comes naturally to us. More naturally than the development of person-to-person relationships. In Bowen's own family and research, he observed that people tended to relate to one another in what he called "clumps."

Take a look at your relationships, and you'll start to see the clumpiness. Maybe you have a group of friends who always get together but never hang out separately. Perhaps you have "couple friends" you only see with your partner. Sometimes the family group chat is the only place a person has interactions with a sibling. Or you may hit "reply all" on an email because it feels less scary than addressing the person who needed the information. (Don't be that person!)

Clumps are one way we maintain emotional distance in relationships. They allow us to communicate with some good social buffering from the group. Social buffering occurs when the presence of a familiar creature or group helps reduce stress. Baby rhesus monkeys respond less fearfully to new situations when a mother or surrogate is present. Cows will lick one another's heads to help lower their heart rate. Humans have the group text, a convenient way to avoid the stress of real human connection (and less messy than head licking).

THE BENEFITS OF CLUMPING:

- Less anxiety
- Fewer awkward silences
- Fuzzy group feelings
- Relays info quickly to many people

THE COSTS OF CLUMPING:

- Fewer close relationships
- Less practice managing anxiety
- More superficial talk
- More dependence on triangles

I'm not writing off groups here. Joining a group is one of the easiest and best ways to improve your overall quality of life. In fact, go join a group right now and come back. What's important is the capacity to build person-to-person relationships *inside* these groups. Without time and attention, our relationships become a little too clumpy in anxious times.

SIGNS OF GROUP CLUMPINESS:

- You only communicate with people in the group text.
- You always sign correspondence from the whole family.
- The group falls apart because two people no longer get along.
- You always need to bring your partner/kids to spend time with your family.
- A group of friends only gathers when everyone can be present.
- You always have both parents on a phone call.
- You only connect with colleagues in group meetings.
- You only relate to extended family through your parents.
- You only provide life updates on social media.
- You need the whole family to participate in therapy (best of luck!).
- Parents always present a "united front" toward a child.

How do you de-clump yourself in a group? You begin to work on developing those person-to-person relationships you learned about in chapter 6. Try making a list of everyone, and rank the quality of relationships from strongest to weakest. Start to look for opportunities to have more emotional contact with them. If beginning with the weakest relationship feels daunting, choose someone in the middle.

If you're an introvert, hear me out. You can be intentional with people without dying of awkwardness. Saying things like "I haven't gotten a chance to hear your thinking about X" or "I feel like I don't know anything about you" are easy ins. Most people love to talk about themselves when given an opportunity. And it doesn't have to be face-to-face in a coffee shop or the break room. Side-by-side conversations, on a walk, or in the car, often can be the most productive.

DEVELOPING PERSON-TO-PERSON RELATIONSHIPS CAN:

1. Increase your own maturity.
2. Make the group more flexible and adaptive.
3. Take the focus off of other people's relationships.

Shriya had a case of the clumps. She relied on her sister to communicate with their mother. She only related to her dad when her mom was present. And her living situation was one giant clump of women. She was also treating her boyfriend like they were a clump, as if he needed to relate to her friends and family exactly the way she did. It never occurred to her that Cam could relate to them in ways she couldn't.

Shriya thought about giving her one-to-one relationships some attention. She needed to spend time with each of her parents without her sister present. She could see the benefit in getting to know her housemates as individuals, without feeling responsible for their interpersonal drama. And she needed to let her boyfriend fly free as he got to know the important people in her life.

ADDING FLAVOR TO OUR RELATIONSHIPS

Most of our relationships are caught in a state of pseudo-connection. When we're too focused on pleasing others, not upsetting them, or keeping them entertained, we suck the flavor right out of them. When they taste like a three-day-old Diet Coke, we're quick to label people as boring or unrelatable. But the problem may be *how* we relate to them.

WE WATER DOWN OUR RELATIONSHIPS BY:

- Always communicating in clumps.
- Spending too much time gossiping.
- Complaining or being critical about others.
- Only relying on superficial topics.
- Only talking about your kids.
- Only sending memes.
- Agreeing when you secretly don't.
- Needing alcohol/drugs to open up.
- Only doing what the other person wants to do.

Look, I get it. I love a meme. And small talk is important. It's a form of social grooming that's essential for group cohesion and to make others feel comfortable. I'm grateful I can ask a friend, "How have you been?" instead of picking through her hair or sniffing her butt to assess her health. But what gets lost in our relationships when we never move past the small talk?

Diving into deeper conversational waters is a tremendous

gift and particular terror. I'm not saying you walk up to somebody after church and say, "Do you really believe that Jesus *rose from the dead*? That's wild!" Or that you ask another parent in the school pickup line, "So what do you think are the qualities of a good education?" But it is kind of surprising how rarely those topics are discussed given the contexts, right?

Look at your life and see where it's time to move past small talk. How can you add some flavor, some depth, some self to key relationships?

WE ADD FLAVOR TO OUR RELATIONSHIPS WHEN WE:

- Work on person-to-person communication.
- Try to understand how people see the world.
- Try to communicate how we've experienced the world.
- Talk about our beliefs, goals, and interests.
- Learn about others' beliefs, goals, and interests.
- Talk about our challenges.
- Learn how someone thinks about their challenges.

It's also useful to stop using perfunctory questions and statements. Here are some examples.

If you always say . . .	Try saying . . .
What's new with you?	What are you excited about these days?
How are you doing?	What's been keeping your brain busy?

I'm doing good.	Let me tell you what I'm excited about.
It's been a stressful week.	Here's what I'm trying to figure out.
We should catch up soon.	Let's find a time to talk so I can hear your thinking about X.

Will people sometimes look at you like you have a third head? That's kind of the point. Sometimes our relationships need a jolt, and people may need a minute to answer your question. But I can't tell you how many federal employees have sighed in relief when I've asked them "What are you excited about?" rather than "What do you do?" at a DC social gathering. Suddenly, a new way of connecting has opened up.

Shriya considered the quality of her person-to-person relationships. Her relationship with Cam was full of flavor because it was new. She was never sure what he would say when they talked about current events or their hopes for the future. But other relationships felt watered down. She used to have great debates with her friends in college, but as working adults they'd settled into ranting about their bosses or quoting TV shows. Shriya realized they weren't very curious about one another anymore.

And then there was her family. Conversations with her mother inevitably led to arguments. Talking to her father felt like having a conversation with a brick wall. She would triangle in her older sister to get out of one-on-one contact with her mother. Perhaps it was time to bring a little courage to her relationships.

SWIM SCHOOL

Have you ever been to a swim class for little kids? There is a messy beauty in watching a pack of toddlers flail and gasp in the water. Much like life, there's a lot of crying, a lot of high-fiving. A lot of parents holding their breath on the sidelines. Everyone has to manage their own anxiety, or it will never work. If a parent rushes in every time a kid cries, they'll never get the chance at mastering the water.

Working on our relationships requires us to manage our anxiety in a more responsible way. We have to acknowledge that we'll get a little wet on the ride, that there will be a lot of awkward stops and starts. And we have to let other people take the plunge. We can't do it for them.

Shriya was in this exact situation with her boyfriend. She was tempted to play the overprotective parent as he braved the waters, navigating the drama and expectations of her friends and family. She told him what topics he'd have to avoid with her more conservative parents. She gave him tips on what excited her friends. She warned him about how they'd responded to boyfriends in the past. Her advice might have kept things temporarily calm, but ultimately she had been getting in Cam's way. It was Cam's responsibility to develop person-to-person relationships with these people. He was a grown man, and this was his challenge, not hers.

Shriya apologized to Cam for her anxious interference. Rather than orchestrating a high-pressure meet and greet, she began to bring Cam along whenever he was interested. Shriya held her breath like a biologist in the field (or a parent at swim class) watching her boyfriend and friends inter-

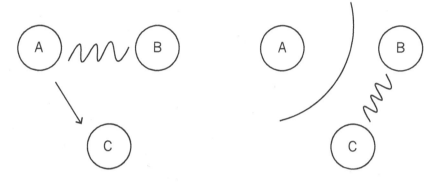

Figure 9. Using triangles to avoid person-to-person relating (left to right). Shriya (A) pulled in her sister (C) when she experienced conflict with their mom. Her sister would scold their mom, and Shriya felt calmer in the outside position. What could it look like for Shriya to begin to relate to people without using the triangle to manage her anxiety?

act. Unsurprisingly, they all acted like grown-ups who could play nice. They discovered their mutual interest in orcas attacking yachts off the coast of Spain. They debated about the best place to get pizza at 2 A.M.

When Shriya finally invited Cam to meet her parents, she tried not to teach him how to interact with them. Instead, she asked him, "Do you have any questions?" And he did have questions about particular cultural norms, and how to be respectful of them. As it turned out, the more freedom and flexibility she gave Cam, the calmer he felt and the less anxiety there was in the room. Cam bonded with her father over their shared love for the James Webb Space Telescope. He was genuinely interested in learning about her mother's exercise routine. Cam could be respectful without playing a part that Shriya had assigned him. Her parents probably liked him better because of it.

CREATING NEW PATHWAYS IN THE BRAIN

Humans are remarkably adaptive. Our super-long infancy and childhood make our brains quite plastic. But we also are masters at believing the exact opposite about ourselves. Somewhere in our childhood most of us got the message that intelligence is fixed, rather than a muscle to be exercised. "Some people are smart, and some aren't" is a lesson that becomes a self-fulfilling prophecy.

When it comes to your relationships, the brain is ready and able to rewire itself. You can create opportunities to observe the power of your brain's neuroplasticity, whether it's learning how to make friends, becoming a parent, or finally telling your mother to stop forwarding body-sculpting coupons. But in order to adapt, we must embrace both success *and* failure in our relationships. We must use the opportunities where we end up overfunctioning, or trying to make everyone happy, to learn something. After all, our blunders help us fine-tune the best way forward. This isn't naïve optimism—it's paying attention to millions of years of evolution.

When we learn something new, the synapses that link our neurons become stronger or weaker. Think about the synaptic connections strengthened by the relationship patterns in your family. Shriya had watched her mother overfunction for her father a million times. She had pulled her sister into her conflict with their mother more times than she could count. She would have to practice being a self many times to strengthen a new pathway in her brain. She couldn't simply make it through one dinner with Cam and her housemates and go, "Got it. He's capable." Approaching her mother one time wouldn't forever dissuade her from triangling in her sister. It would be an ongoing effort to be more differentiated.

But every time Shriya could sit back, letting her boyfriend be himself with her roommates, she was challenging her brain's assumption that he wasn't capable. Every time she could talk to her sister about her own life, rather than her frustration with their mother, she became a little less reliant on the triangle. Another flavor of relating would begin to open up. Her brain, and the relationship system, would learn.

A DAUGHTER'S EMOTIONAL COURAGE

Shriya was making strides in her relationships with her boyfriend and friends. She was strengthening new connections in her brain. But she couldn't forget about the final bosses waiting at the end—her parents. Shriya wanted stronger relationships with them as well. But the fusion in these relationships, the sensitivity to her parents' potential upsetness, was so high, it was difficult to see a way forward. Shriya's mind went blank whenever she tried to carry a conversation with her father. And it felt impossible to be curious about her mother, who was constantly interrupting Shriya. When her mom tried to overfunction for her, Shriya would give in, or lecture her mother about being too overbearing. A lot was being said, but little was being communicated.

Relating to her parents in a less predictable way, one that was less about quickly managing anxiety, would require a great deal of emotional courage. Emotional courage is a willingness to tolerate the distress that comes with putting your best thinking into action.

- Hanging in a conversation when you want to run away.
- Ending a conversation when a boundary needs to be set.
- Asking questions to get at a person's thinking.
- Taking a deep breath when you want to interrupt.
- Setting boundaries when a person tries to over-function.
- Sharing your thinking without lecturing or bullying.

Plugging these examples into a single conversation would be like spinning six plates simultaneously. So Shriya tried to find *one* opportunity with each of her parents to switch things up. One small step toward differentiation of self in these relationships. She started by taking her mother out to lunch. When she ordered French fries, her mother scolded her about the lack of vegetables on her plate. Shriya took a deep breath and said, "Mom, I'm not interested in discussing my eating habits right now. If I need advice, I will ask you. Now let me tell you what's going on with me." Her mother frowned, but didn't say anything. She was taking it all in.

Encouraged by the success, Shriya tried another strategy with her father. She composed an email, pretending she was giving a life update to a close friend. She talked about her excitement about her relationship with Cam. Her goals for her career. Her reactions to various stories in the news that challenged her thinking. Rather than sending the email (way too scary!), she printed it out. And she kept it in front of her when she called her father once a week. When he asked her how she was doing, she suddenly had some answers. By considering the person-to-person relating she might do with a friend, she began to relate to her dad as an individual, not just the quiet half of her parents' marriage.

A few things were happening here. Shriya was teaching her brain that her parents' anxiety was not hers to manage. She also was showing herself that she was capable of courage in these relationships. Her parents could see that she wasn't going anywhere, but she was also unwilling to operate the way she once had.

Does this mean Shriya's mother stopped interfering in her daughter's choices? That she never rolled her eyes at a cupcake ever again? Or that her father never answered her earnest stories with dead silence? Of course not. Differentiation is not about others. It is about self.

Like Shriya, some people have the privilege of being in families that are more tolerant of our moves toward differentiation (even if they aren't thrilled about them). While for others, the reactivity may be so high that people may threaten to end contact with you. You may find that you need to restructure contact with them or set clearer boundaries in the relationship. But when we work on differentiation of self, we give both ourselves and the relationship a fighting chance to be something different. When we hop off the Ferris wheel, we create the possibility of a new adventure with the people we love.

Shriya was making space to be surprised by others. She was surprised by how well her boyfriend managed himself with her friends and family. And she was shocked that she still had things to learn about her parents. Above all, she was surprised by herself. Shriya was learning to be a person who could be authentic and not spontaneously combust. A person excited by the possibilities in her relationships.

EXERCISE 1: **Dump the clump.** What are the relationship clumps in your life that need untangling? A gossipy work environment? A friend group where nobody hangs out one-on-one? A family that only gives updates in the group text? Make a plan to single out one or two people in each of these clumps. How can you make time to strengthen these person-to-person relationships?

EXERCISE 2: **Taste the rainbow.** Which relationships in your life lack some flavor? When have you been quick to write people off as uninteresting or unengaging? Consider how you can give these relationships a jolt of flavor by asking questions you normally wouldn't ask, or sharing things about yourself without as much anxious editing. Pretend you're hanging out with a good friend, and just be yourself.

EXERCISE 3: **Teach your brain new tricks.** When it comes to your relationships, what are the well-trod pathways in your brain? Is it the tendency to make everyone feel comfortable? The impulse to ramble when nervous? The habit of hiding when invited to go out? It's time to give your brain a chance to do something new—to learn that there's more than one way to relate to people. What are the lessons you can learn, even as an adult?

CHAPTER NUGGETS

- People often relate to one another in clumps rather than on a person-to-person level.
- Social buffering is the way the presence of familiar creatures or groups helps reduce stress.
- Relationship clumps can help manage anxiety and awkwardness, but they can also keep us from developing person-to-person relationships with people who are important to us.
- De-clumping your relationships can help increase your maturity and add more flexibility to the group.
- Many of our relationships are in a state of watered-down pseudo-connection. To add flavor and depth to your relationships, try asking questions that aren't the default small talk that invites perfunctory answers.
- The emotional process in your family reinforces certain pathways in the brain. We can rewire our brains by operating with more emotional courage in relationships.
- Emotional courage is a willingness to tolerate the distress that comes with putting your best thinking into action.

12

LEARNING TO EVALUATE OURSELVES

"I would ask what I would bring, but I already know that I'm enough."

—Ava Coleman, *Abbott Elementary*

WHEN PEOPLE ASKED Rachel how she was doing, she had no idea what to say. If you looked at her social media, you'd guess she was a happy, somewhat disheveled Presbyterian minister who loved her two kids. If you asked her husband, he'd say she was way too hard on herself. Her six-year-old daughter would say, "Mommy moves around like her butt's on fire." And her three-year-old son would make aggressive truck noises.

Since her second child had arrived, Rachel felt stuck in survival mode. Everyone had told her that kid number two would be easier—she wouldn't second-guess herself, or focus too much on every parenting detail. Nothing had been further from the truth. Around the time she went back to work, she'd fallen down an Instagram rabbit hole. She'd hide in her office during lunch, shoving a sad-looking salad in her face while she scrolled endlessly. She wasn't sure what she was looking for, but the algorithm silently noted what she stopped and studied.

Rachel's not-so-secret obsession was Mormon momfluencers, cheerful frontier women who homeschooled their kids and still had time to retile the kitchen backsplash. She watched women fill giant mason jars with bespoke healthy snacks. They put on flawless makeup in the Chick-fil-A drive-through. They helped their twenty-seven children make "Christ-centered art" without getting a spot of paint on their buttery-soft athleisure wear. She didn't *want* this life. But she did feel guilty when she tossed bags of Doritos into the back of the minivan or turned on cartoons after a long day. And honestly, who wouldn't love a new backsplash?

For the first time, Rachel found herself doubting her gifts as a pastor. It didn't help that her evaluation had just dropped. Some people wanted her to "smile more" when she greeted new visitors. Others were put off by her lack of availability in the evenings. One older gentleman offered to email her a weekly critique of her sermon. She congratulated herself for not immediately upturning the tables Jesus-style.

Some critiques were plain old misogyny, but some of them started to creep into her brain. It didn't help that the church had a new youth pastor, a twenty-five-year-old fresh out of seminary. Michael had the unencumbered confidence of someone who hadn't yet been dragged by Barbara, the seventy-five-year-old church administrator, for excessive copy machine use. Or brought in to mediate an argument about which picture of white Jesus should hang in the foyer (none of them!). Michael was loved, he had energy, and he had exactly zero children. Rather than see him as a resource, the red lights began to flash in Rachel's brain. *Danger. Danger.*

How was she really doing? Rachel managed her anxiety by relying on her husband for reassurance that she was a great mom and pastor. "You have to stop asking me that," her husband said one night before bed. "It doesn't seem like I can convince you that you're amazing." She was very pissed at this response, but in her heart she knew he was right. She would have to find a different way to evaluate herself.

GROWING QUESTIONS

Humans are fantastically terrible at evaluating ourselves. In Western cultures, people are often too optimistic when it comes to their abilities. A majority of workers at a company will think they're performing in the top 5 percent. Teens who think they are very knowledgeable about birth control are more likely to get pregnant. Elderly drivers who think they're very competent are more likely to get in an accident. Our peers tend to be much better at evaluating us than we are.

As optimistic as we may be about skills, we also careen toward intense self-criticism. A hundred years ago, you only had to compare yourself to your neighbors. Now, thanks to social media, we're flooded with examples of success, beauty, and "optimal living" from all corners of the world. It's no surprise that anxiety and depression rates keep rising, in particular among teenage girls.

Few schools teach or encourage kids to give self-evaluations of their progress. Yet we expect adults to be able to give themselves thoughtful evaluations as an employee, a partner, or a parent. When I ask a therapy client to evaluate themselves, they often use a lot of binary language. There's a tendency to label behavior as good or bad, healthy or unhealthy, functional or dysfunctional, productive or lazy. But if the cultural definitions of words like "healthy," "productive," and "successful" are damn near impossible to achieve, no wonder people feel that they come up short.

Perhaps we are terrible at evaluating ourselves because we're asking the wrong questions. Questions that promote self-comparison are relationship oriented in nature. They use words like "should," "ought," "must," "enough," etc. They are questions that trigger avoidance, accommodation, or even acting out. They are not what I call "growing questions." Growing questions spark curiosity, flexibility, and creativity. They reflect more than an anxious borrowing of values or standards. To get you started, I've included a long list of growing questions at the end of the book. But I'd encourage you to create your own.

Anxious Questions	Growing Questions
Am I doing enough?	How would I like to be responsible?
How might I screw this up?	How do I react when stress is high?
Am I doing as well as everyone else?	Where have I seen progress?
What will get people's attention?	What is important to me?
What might upset people?	What are the challenges I face?
Is it too late for me to do this?	How do I face challenges with maturity?

Some may label these anxious questions as negative thinking patterns. This may be true, but they are also fingerprints of group pressure, the tendency toward togetherness that promotes social cohesion. You learned in earlier chapters that we've evolved to mimic higher-ranking group members for good reasons. You see Cady Heron wearing army pants and flip-flops, so you buy army pants and flip-flops. It's funny, and a little sad, but it's also an incredibly useful adaptation. When stress is high, we copy people to get by and not cause a stir. Mentally, you can beat yourself up about it, or you can take a deep breath and ask some growing questions instead.

Rachel thought about the questions she used to evaluate herself. Questions like, "Am I as put together as other women with two kids? How should my house look? Do members of the congregation seem happy? Did my sermon get as many laughs as Michael's?" These are questions that generate a sense of urgency. An urgency that had made her borrow answers from her friends, her congregation, or—cue ominous music—the internet.

ENOUGH WITH "ENOUGH"

"Enough" is a word that plagues our society. Am I working hard enough? Am I being a good enough friend? Am I taking care of my body enough to live long enough? Am I doing enough to help as a daughter, a community member, a citizen of the globe? Who the heck knows.

Until you have a reasoned, realistic definition of who you're trying to be in the world, the word "enough" will continue to creep into your thinking. You'll continue to evaluate yourself based on:

- How you feel.
- The reactions of others.
- The values of others.

Three ever-changing variables! So if you feel like a bad partner, you conclude that you must be one. If Bob from accounting thinks you aren't ready for a promotion, this must be true. If your neighbor keeps a tidy yard, you better get out the hedge clippers.

Intellectually, we know that feelings fluctuate. Society has responded by trying to normalize these feelings. Everyone has imposter syndrome! Every mother has mommy guilt! So don't sweat it! By anxiously swatting them away, we lose sight of how these emotions do impact our functioning and our relationships. If you had a parent who felt "less than" in their parenting, their appearance, or their career success, this likely had an impact on you. The anxiety is contagious.

I'm not saying this to make you feel guilty for feeling guilty, or to feel anxious about feeling anxious. I'm simply suggesting that anxious reactions to being human can generate more trouble than our actual shortcomings. For example, would you rather have a boss who was constantly worried they weren't supporting you enough, or one who was okay with the reality that sometimes they fell short? A friend who occasionally forgets to call you back, or one who is anxiously focused on being a "good friend"? It's an interesting question, right?

When we don't feel good enough, we often end up managing our anxiety with the same predictable patterns. We freeze up, unable to make any changes, we throw a lot of energy at the problem and burn out quickly, or we just do whatever others tell us to do. There is little to no self in any of these responses.

SITUATION: You don't have a lot of time to exercise.
REACTION: You give up entirely because you can't have the body of a fitness influencer.

SITUATION: You feel like your boss is disappointed in you.
REACTION: You copy whatever your colleagues are doing that seems to make them happy.

SITUATION: You feel like you're not invested enough in your child's education.
REACTION: You sign them up for a bunch of expensive math and science camps you can't afford.

These are not grown-up solutions. They're akin to grabbing a fire extinguisher and blasting the crap out of our self-doubt. The fire might be out, but you've created an entirely new mess. Generating solutions that reflect your principles and beliefs is a much slower process. You have to tolerate some discomfort as you make choices that may differ from your peers'. Choices that might not always please the boss.

Rachel thought about the moments when she didn't feel good enough. She tended to have these thoughts late at night, after a day when she'd accidentally rolled the stroller through dog poop or spent too much time on social media. At night, she was more vulnerable to making a quick, peer-influenced decision about how to live her life. Perhaps she didn't need to summon an objective, reasoned view of her life at 10 P.M. So she decided to refrain from any evaluation at all after 7 P.M. Night would be for slowing down, calming down in ways that didn't involve buying parenting books on Amazon, scrolling through social media, or venting to her husband. Instead, Rachel tried to read a novel, say a prayer, or watch Scandinavian detectives solve grisly murders.

This is what it looks like to begin to take responsibility for your own distress. To look at the quick solutions and distractions the culture offers and say, "No thanks, I'm good." By managing our anxiety more responsibly, we give ourselves a chance to evaluate ourselves with clarity and kindness.

SUPERMARKET SWEEP

As a cable TV child of the nineties, I watched a lot of the game show *Supermarket Sweep*. For the show's final challenge, contestants raced their shopping carts through the staged grocery store, trying to rack up the highest dollar amount. Giant turkeys, steaks, and diapers flew off the shelves as the audience roared.

I can't think of a better analogy for modern life. The more uncertain we are, the more quickly we shove the world's values into our cart. Life becomes about accumulating status, wealth, or the "right" beliefs as fast as possible, with few people stopping to look at the labels. Instagram likes? Sure. Trendy parenting strategies? Gimme. Impossible body or productivity standards? Fill her up.

This is the pseudo-self at work. In the absence of our own measures and beliefs, we snatch the most convenient ones. How we compare to others. What ranks higher in the algorithm. What keeps the most people happy. Many of these beliefs are simply unattainable. Yet people continue to believe the self-help gurus who tell them to wake up at 5 A.M. We tell ourselves, *Today is the day I will become a productivity machine, immune to exhaustion, distraction, and stress eating!* Fast-forward sixteen hours, and you've just destroyed a block of Vermont cheddar in bed while researching the cast of *Smallville* on Wikipedia.

Often the most convenient measures we use for ourselves are the least flexible ones. They are rigid, unimaginative, and frankly kind of a hilarious. And they certainly aren't kind.

CONVENIENT, RIGID MEASURES:

- Did everyone like my social media post?
- Did people laugh at my jokes, or nod enthusiastically when I was talking?
- Do I feel successful?
- Does my house look like no one lives here?
- Does my kid never scream or pout?
- Do I eat zero processed food?
- Do I have the energy of a twenty-five-year-old?
- Do I look like an actress who's just emerged from hair and makeup?

KIND, FLEXIBLE MEASURES:

- Did I refrain from any assholery?
- Did I get fresh air today?
- Did I try to be present with people and listen to them?
- Did I try to manage some of my anxiety?

- Did I let myself be delighted by something?
- Did I make space for good thinking?
- Was I honest about what I could and couldn't do?
- How did I try to be a responsible human today?

Nothing on that first list is going to make you feel secure for longer than a day or two. Greater maturity, kindness, and curiosity may not produce instant results, but they provide a more solid foundation for growth. Though the culture may say otherwise, we cannot move through life at the speed of a game show. For a species built to keep up with the group, shifting out of this mind-set can be daunting. But it is a survivable kind of anxiety. One that has a lot to teach us.

Rachel knew that her standards for evaluating herself were impossible, unappetizing, and comical. She had stopped inviting friends to her house because it wasn't Instagram worthy. When she tried to act like an enlightened Montessori teacher with her kids, she grew frustrated and surrendered the iPad to them. She caught herself trying to copy Michael's speaking style at church, which made her sermons sound disjointed and confusing. Her life had become a collage of other people's values and efforts. No wonder it felt alien to her.

THE CONVENIENCE OF SELF-COMPARISON

Self-comparison is a convenient measure. It's a quick way to temporarily boost our mood and functioning without much effort. Upward social comparison can motivate us to achieve more. Downward social comparison can help us feel better about ourselves. If they didn't, we probably wouldn't have so much mommy shaming, internet bullying, or celebrity worship in our world. The more anxious you are, the more quickly you may find that you're using someone else as a yardstick.

CONVENIENT MEASURES OF SELF-COMPARISON:

- How well your siblings are doing.
- How much praise your colleagues get.
- Everyone's social media feed.
- How well your high school classmates are doing.
- What everyone else is wearing, eating, buying.
- How busy everyone else is.

These measures are quick and convenient. But they don't necessarily nourish us or help us grow. They just keep us hungry. They keep us scrambling toward things we may not value. They keep us subscribed to ideas we don't actually believe.

I'm not sure that you can teach a person not to self-compare. Evolution installed this button for a good reason. I try to think of self-comparison as sort of a "check engine" light. It can signal a deficit in one's own principles and beliefs. A lack of a more solid system of self-evaluation. We all have arenas in life where we're less likely to self-compare than others. Maybe you feel less self-conscious about your appearance as you've gotten older, or you feel more secure in your decision to not drink alcohol. This is probably because you have built up more solid self in this arena—you've done good thinking about what you believe and are trying to do.

Asking good questions can help you shift from pseudo-self to solid self. From anxious self-comparison to a life guided by your own principles.

PSEUDO-SELF: How many of my friends are married already?
SOLID SELF: How am I trying to function in dating/relationships?

PSEUDO-SELF: Does my boss praise me as much as they praise others?
SOLID SELF: How do I think I've been doing at work? What's worth paying attention to?

PSEUDO-SELF: Can my kid do everything his peers can do?
SOLID SELF: How would I like to relate to my child as he navigates life's challenges?

PSEUDO-SELF: Everyone in the universe is at the beach this week, except for me.
SOLID SELF: How would I like to have a meaningful, joyful day?

Rachel thought about how she used self-comparison to boost her mood and functioning.

She often compared her parenting victories to others' supposed failures. On their date nights, she and her husband would frequently swap stories about wild things they'd seen other parents do. They'd congratulate themselves, only to have self-doubt creep in the next day. Though she hated to admit it, Rachel noticed that she felt better about herself when her other clergy friends were struggling. She felt more confident, more optimistic about her professional future immediately after Michael dropped the ball on a task. She didn't want her functioning to depend on other people's failures any more than she wanted to feel like crap when others were crushing life. She wanted off this terrible ride that didn't promote much empathy or joy for others.

NEEDING PERMISSION TO BE HUMAN

Don't you just love it when people talk about their imperfections? When a writer says they don't write every day, my body instantly relaxes. When a celebrity admits they too love Burger King, they get a congratulatory "Stars! They're just like us!" headline. During the pandemic, listening to people talk about their lack of productivity was like crawling under a warm, cozy blanket. We all sleep better when we're reminded that people are . . . people.

Telling people not to be too hard on themselves is a multimillion-dollar, if not billion-dollar, industry. Anti-hustle culture has become increasingly popular, existing in kind of a symbiotic relationship with the gurus who shame you for relaxing. We buy books that tell us to wake up at 5 A.M., and then we listen to podcasts criticizing the people who tell us to wake up at 5 A.M. It is all deeply satisfying, because we get the dopamine hit from thinking about changing, and we get the dopamine hit from feeling superior to the very people who gave us that advice.

Perhaps the problem isn't that we're simply too hard on ourselves. Maybe it's also that we need people to tell us this. Accepting the culture and rejecting the culture can both be flavors of relationship orientation, both anxious reactions. When anxiety goes up, so does the need to borrow self. You need look no further than the self-care industry to see this. Yes, there is a place for these messages. But people also can know their own minds. You can look at the facts and determine the best way forward without needing permission from an expert or a hashtag. Without seeing that someone else has come to the same determination as you.

Self-evaluation is a muscle that strengthens with exercise and atrophies without it. And a person who engages in more self-evaluation more freely moves into self-expression. In other words, they can give themselves permission to be as they are. And they can more easily let others be themselves. The more "self" you put in your choices, the less discomfort you'll probably experience when people make different choices. People might have a fourth kid, move to Australia, wake up at 5 A.M., or take up professional boogie boarding without you having to ask yourself, "Should I be doing that too?" You're also freer to make your own choices that depart from the group. You can be the one friend who has beautiful neck wrinkles, the parent who doesn't let their kid have a smartphone, or the grandpa who intimately knows the choreography of BTS.

MORE SOLID SELF EQUALS:

- More comfort with differences.
- More belief-driven behavior.
- Less of a need for others to follow.
- Less of a need to follow others.
- Less likely to be influenced by others' reactions.
- Less likely to be influenced by the feelings of the moment.

Rachel began to pay attention to all the ways she sought permission for her actions. She had googled, "A little screen time won't damage your kid." She had scoured the memoirs of female clergy. She'd listened to podcasts about body positivity. She studied the people in her life with small incomes who were very happy. There was nothing wrong with these actions. But there was very little of her own thinking in these decisions. The bulk of her data was other people's opinions and experiences. How could her own thinking play a bigger role?

When Rachel paid more attention to how anxiety influenced her decisions, she began to think differently about her growth. A simple change of behavior wasn't the goal. She needed to overhaul *how* she made decisions. In other words, she didn't need to find the best parenting book to be a good mom. She needed to set aside a few minutes every week to do good thinking about parenting. She didn't need the perfect couch to tie the living room together. She needed to ask herself how she wanted to enjoy her home. By thinking about the process of evaluation, she opened up space for more creativity and curiosity. Perhaps there was more than one way to be an excellent parent. To create a welcoming space for friends. To pastor a congregation.

This wisdom didn't need to be as long as a sermon. Rachel knew that the best thinking could fit on a sticky note. "Slow down and be present" ended up being more of a helpful principle than a twenty-page manifesto on child-rearing. "Did you ask good questions?" was a more useful evaluation for sermons than the most detailed hermeneutical critique.

The tendency to borrow self was always there. Rachel admitted that it would always be easier to absorb momfluencer content than think about her own principles for relating to her kids. It would always be easier to shove things quickly into closets than invite people into her wholehearted messy life. She could feel good about herself when Michael flailed, or she could untether herself and live out her own calling. Because her church didn't need another Michael. And her kids didn't need a seemingly perfect mother, someone who color coordinated their outfits or made her own potpourri. They needed a mother who could handle the slow and steady work of becoming a grown-up. One who could show them that messes, setbacks, and failure were manageable parts of life.

Slowly, Rachel was learning to develop and trust her own thinking. She was starting to see her colleague as a gift, not her competition. She started putting down her phone at lunch, saying a quick prayer for all the moms in the world. Yes, even the ones in buttery-soft athleisure. And when she was tempted to turn over in bed at night, asking her husband, "I'm doing okay, right?"—she let him sleep. She knew what she was about.

EXERCISE 1: **Hoop jumping.** When do you tend to hyper-focus on societal definitions of success? Through what impossible hoops are you trying to drag your tired, anxious butt? Is it making every moment of your kid's day educational? Reading dense Russian novels instead of your favorite cozy mysteries? Reaching a ridiculous weight goal, or learning to do something that has never once brought you an ounce of joy? What are some kinder measures you can use? What's a flexible, realistic definition of what a good day looks like for you?

EXERCISE 2: **Quick comparison.** Think about how you use quick comparisons to manage distress. Do you check everyone's wardrobe at work? Do you gossip about other people's failures? Do you let someone's accomplishments be proof of your own "laziness"? Choose one particular topic, like health, parenting, career, relationships, hobbies, etc. and try to outline some of your own wisdom. Does any of this thinking depart from public opinion or the popular culture?

EXERCISE 3: **Your permission slip.** Where do you look to others' imperfections or reassurances to give yourself permission to be human? How can you do more of this work yourself? Create and print out your own permission slip to be whatever you need to be. Imperfect, a work in progress, a human, a child of God, etc.—use whatever words you need to use to remember who you are.

CHAPTER NUGGETS

- Humans are not great at evaluating ourselves. We tend to overestimate our abilities, or sink into self-criticism.

- Anxious, relationship-oriented questions are not questions that help us grow as individuals. Growing questions help us be more purposeful and true to ourselves. They help us to think about how we want to be more responsible for ourselves.

- Worrying about whether you are doing "enough" can lead you to evaluate yourself based on your current feelings. It can also lead you to anxious fixing that does not increase maturity.

- The more uncertain you feel, the more likely you will borrow the culture's definitions of success. These are often rigid measures that aren't kind, and don't reflect our best thinking.

- We use self-comparison to motivate ourselves and manage our anxiety. Developing your own principles for life can help you self-evaluate without needing to self-compare.

- It can be useful to focus on how you make decisions, not just the content of your decisions. Rather than looking for permission to be yourself, make space to define your own thinking about who you'd like to be.

13

FINDING THE COURAGE TO TAKE A POSITION

"If there is any dirty trick I cannot stand, it is honesty."
—Amy Brookheimer, *Veep*

DONNA LOVED HER children, but she relished being an empty nester. She had survived a nasty divorce when they were younger, and her proudest accomplishment was launching them into the world. She had looked forward to the future, imagining herself traveling the globe, meeting mysterious men, and never doing anyone else's laundry ever again. She could not have been more wrong.

Three years after the last kid had moved out, Donna had shocked everyone, including herself a little, by marrying a woman. Jane was a natural complement to Donna's loud, boisterous self. She was quiet, independent, and perfect, except for one teensy complication. She came with a boarder, her thirty-year-old daughter Annie.

When Annie asked to move in for "a bit" after losing her job, Donna assumed this meant a few months. One year in, and Annie wasn't going anywhere. She hadn't found a job, and she'd barricaded herself in her room, emerging only to raid the fridge, take long baths, or lecture them about the ills of late-stage capitalism. "Money means nothing to me," she'd say as she kicked back one of Donna's beers.

Jane wasn't oblivious to The Annie Problem. But her relationship with her daughter had always been tense. Jane worried that if she started enforcing some rules, Annie would run away to her other mom, Jane's ex-wife. So her best strategy for keeping things calm was some good old emotional distance—pretending there wasn't a problem.

Occasionally, Annie emerged from her bunker to join them for dinner, when she'd start a political rant. Her latest fixation was the neighbors, who opposed the city's latest project to put a bike lane down their street. Bloodred "We need parking!" signs littered their yards, and they'd been pestering Donna to put one on hers. Donna didn't own a bike, but parking a block or two away from her house didn't set her blood boiling. She had bigger worries at home.

One afternoon Donna came home to find a cardboard sign sticking out of her flower bed. At first she thought a neighbor had taken liberties, but upon further inspection, she saw that the homemade sign read, "Down with NIMBY fascists!"

Absolutely livid, Donna ripped the sign out of the dirt. She was done with politics, and done with Annie. Someone was moving out of the house, and it wasn't going to be her.

IRRESPONSIBLY OVERINVOLVED

We live in a yard-sign world. One that constantly demands us to take a position. Thanks to social media algorithms and rage-based media, we are more aware of daily terrors than we've ever been. Silence feels like a dangerous acceptance of the status quo, but generating a response to every tragedy, every school shooting and natural disaster, feels overwhelming. No wonder people feel burned out and hopeless in this time of great anxiety.

In the bigness of the world's problems, I always go back to the family. The family is a microcosm of society, and societal anxiety gets managed in a similar way as family anxiety. Thinking about the family system can help a person slow down, think, and not be surprised by how communities respond to stress on a bigger scale.

So in times of great stress, what do families do?

- They become less flexible.
- They distance and avoid talking about the issues.
- Some people become over-responsible for others.
- Some people begin to underfunction.
- They find a convenient scapegoat.
- They focus on quick fixes and symptom relief.
- They struggle to define and implement principle-based solutions.
- They focus on feeling-oriented solutions rather than thoughtful ones.

Did I just describe American politics, your workplace, or your family? Perhaps all of the above? Whether you're looking at organizational, neighborhood, or national politics, you're likely to see similar attempts to manage stress. Often they are more about relieving the anxiety of the moment than finding the best way forward.

I don't think that Bowen theory is the answer to every

problem. But I cannot overstate the usefulness of having a theory to think about human behavior. Not to excuse it, but to watch the patterns at play. One societal pattern I've observed recently is overfunctioning, the tendency to be over-involved in others' responses to crises. We try to lend self to others because it is more comfortable. It is easier to lecture people on social media or at the dinner table. It is much harder to stay plugged in to challenges as your most responsible self.

Bowen wrote, "A person working toward responsibility in self is always aware of his responsibility to others. As he devotes primary energy to self, he automatically becomes more responsible toward others, and less irresponsibly over-involved with others."

Often we confuse being responsible with being "irresponsibly overinvolved" with others. Railing on your parents for their opinions about climate change is not responsibility, any more than making fun of people who pray is taking a position on gun control. From a Bowen theory perspective, these are reactions, not positions. They are attempts to manage one's own reactivity by attacking others. A position is a step we take to be more responsibly involved with a challenge.

Annie probably thought she was taking a position when she slammed the yard sign into Donna's zinnias. And maybe she was. Donna suspected, however, that the sign was more about pissing off the neighbors than getting a political outcome. The trouble was, Donna was tempted to respond with the same level of immaturity. She found herself engaging in caustic debate with Annie at the dinner table, while Jane sat quietly. She found herself reading articles about progressive capitalism simply to have bombs to chuck at her stepdaughter every evening. You can imagine how well this went over.

Getting nowhere with Annie, Donna turned her emotional tentacles toward Jane. She tried coaching her wife on how to be firmer with her daughter. She suggested ways to ask Annie to pay rent or put her dishes in the dishwasher. Jane would have moments of courage in talking to Annie, but she abandoned her efforts as soon as Annie failed to follow through with her promises. Donna's irresponsible overinvolvement with Jane led to tension in the marriage. They weren't on the brink of divorce, but Donna's focus on Annie and Jane's relationship certainly weakened her own person-to-person relationship with Jane.

Donna knew that things couldn't continue as they were. Arguing with Annie at dinner wasn't getting her anywhere. Lecturing Jane about how to parent wasn't working. But neither was going along with the status quo. How could Donna be more responsible for herself in these challenges?

NO-SELF QUICK FIXES

When anxiety is high, we use relationship pressure as our compass. We know that responses that deviate from the norm may not be tolerated. Afraid of being called out, some people may accommodate, adopting the actions, the emotionality, and the urgency of those around us. Those more disagreeable in nature may act out, rebelling simply to invite conflict. Others avoid the issue altogether, and hope no one notices. The three As are just as present in the societal patterns as they are in the family. Accommodating, acting out, and avoiding are "no-self" positions wrapped in different packaging.

Think about how you've responded to family, community, or even national crises and challenges in the past few years.

YOU MIGHT HAVE:

- Distanced because the problem felt too complex.
- Distanced because the anxiety was too high.
- Become overinvolved in telling other people how to respond.
- Automatically borrowed the beliefs and behaviors of others.
- Spent the bulk of your energy criticizing others.
- Acted quickly and randomly to feel better.
- Attacked the problem until you burned out.

I don't know about you, but I'm seven for seven.

Some of these behaviors can be quite effective in moments of crisis. Our tendency toward togetherness can help us activate plans quickly and efficiently. But what happens when we get stuck in sporadic, quick-fixing reactions? For one, we put ourselves at risk of not addressing root causes that produce the symptoms of a crisis. We also tend to be more focused on reactions that resolve our immediate anxiety than thoughtful responses.

Fast reactions from the group can scare people into behaving better. The togetherness force can dissuade people from giving in to their antisocial, selfish desires. Without this relationship pressure, society wouldn't function.

But as far as I know, no one has ever been pressured, pulled, or bullied into greater maturity.

You are the only person you can bring into maturity. This requires time, energy, and a great deal of discomfort. In tense moments, the togetherness force keeps us focused on what everyone else is doing, or what they should be doing. There is less tolerance for people finding their own way to address the community's or the world's problems. And it's harder to be curious about the challenges.

In Donna's house, there was little to no self in anyone's reactions. Donna had been anxiously accommodating Jane's parenting style for an entire year. Jane was avoiding standing up to her daughter, and Annie was acting out, regressing to her teenage self. Annie might have looked like the least mature of the three of them, but no one was focused on their own responsibility. Nobody was bringing any self to the table. They were all stuck in their automatic, emotional reactions.

Donna considered that she hadn't brought much maturity to the bike lane controversy either. She'd avoided her neighbors, not wanting to take a stance on the issue. And now she was tempted to act out, opposing the bike lane just to piss off Annie. She knew there was a better way, both in her response to the dilemma and in her relationship challenges with Annie. But it would take a lot more time and effort.

SITTING DOWN FOR YOUR BELIEFS

Western culture loves the idea of standing up for your beliefs. Will you do what's right when your beliefs are tested? Will you speak up when you see something wrong? When social media algorithms amplify the loudest, angriest voices, we end up with a narrow version of this ideal. Standing up ends up looking a lot like clapping back.

Sometimes we skip over an important part of defining one's self—sitting down. Before you stand up for beliefs, you have to *have* beliefs. It's hard to do the standing if you haven't done the sitting—the thoughtful work of figuring out what you think.

SITTING DOWN FOR YOUR BELIEFS CAN LOOK LIKE:

- Educating yourself.
- Building relationships with people who have relevant knowledge/experiences.
- Defining your own beliefs based on reason, evidence, and values.
- Being open to changing beliefs based on new evidence/experience.
- Being thoughtful about opportunities to activate this thinking.

Sitting down isn't staying down. It's not burying yourself in "education" so you never have to take a position. That's distancing disguised as maturity.

How much sitting down have you done for important arenas in your life? How much time have you spent defining your beliefs about being a parent? A partner? A person on this planet? Sometimes sitting down and writing a few paragraphs about your own thinking feels self-indulgent or incredibly boring. But isn't that strange, considering the time we dedicate to less serious tasks? Maybe you spent three hours one night following the Harry Styles "spit-gate" (me!), but just asked a friend who to vote for in the mayoral race. A parent might spend ten hours trying to get their teenager

Taylor Swift tickets and zero minutes developing their thinking about how to raise a teenager. As someone who loves an internet rabbit hole, I'm not trying to make you feel bad, only suggesting that there might be more time for thinking than we might realize.

For some, however, having time to develop one's beliefs is a privilege. Many people in the world live in a state of chaotic urgency. Their survival depends on their quick reactions. But if you have the time and ability to think about complex problems, how can you use this privilege responsibly? The world needs people who are able to stay plugged in to problems longer than the news cycle. It needs responders, not just reactors.

Donna was a busy woman. She couldn't descend into a cave for three weeks and emerge fully informed about urban development and the Annie situation. But she needed to dedicate some solo time for thinking. And she also needed to reach out to others. Rather than looking for the loudest voices, Donna decided to contact people who had stayed plugged in to neighborhood problems over the long haul. She emailed the neighborhood commissioner to hear her thinking. She talked with a friend who rode his bike around the city, listening to his experiences dealing with drivers. She brought cookies to a neighbor with mobility challenges and listened to her concerns about the bike lane. And she thought about what kind of city she wanted to live in.

Donna also decided she needed to increase her contact with Annie. Not to debate economic policy, but to get to know her specific interests and challenges. How could Donna respond to the family challenge if she didn't know the person the decision affected? One night she knocked on Annie's door, jingling her car keys. "If you're going to drink my beer," she told Annie, "then you're going to help me pick it out." This was the first of many late-night runs to the grocery store, when Donna tried to get to know her stepdaughter.

MINI-STEPS AND MINI-POSITIONS

When you first read the title of this chapter, what images came to mind? Did you think of Nelson Mandela or Malala Yousafzai? Sally Field standing on a table in *Norma Rae*? When we think of courage, we often think of cinema-worthy moments when everyone's eyes are on the protagonist. It's easy to overlook the smaller, day-to-day moments when you have an opportunity to live out your thinking. To define yourself to others and be less guided by relationship pressure. This could look like moving toward someone you'd like to avoid. To not let a hurtful comment slip by unnoticed at the dinner table. To not cancel at the last moment when you promised you'd show up.

Bowen described differentiation as a series of mini-steps. A series of mini-positions we take based on our own thinking. Let's say that one of your principles is to honor the commitments you make. Then you'd better think twice before you say yes to anything, because each "yes" is a small but important position.

A MINI-POSITION COULD LOOK LIKE:

- Setting and holding boundaries in important relationships.
- Living out your definitions of respect and love for others.
- Moving toward someone you used to avoid.

- Speaking up in a room full of people who disagree.
- Setting aside time for personal goals.

Emotional courage is not an absence of distress or fear, nor is it a desire to piss people off. Some of the people we label as courageous might actually be very driven by others' reactions, positive or negative. Some people get a kick out of being disagreeable, while others feel they must win the room over. Like differentiation, emotional courage has nothing to do with other people's reactions.

Donna realized that she'd been focused on big positions and not the small but important ones. She was asking herself constantly, *Should I let Annie live here? Should I support the bike lane?* But now she saw that she was already on the right path, taking one mini-step at a time. Every conversation with a neighbor, and every grocery store run with Annie, she was getting a little closer to finding these answers. She wasn't sure she was always doing the "next right thing," but she could try her best to do the next *thoughtful* thing.

One day, Donna made a not-so-mini step. She went to Jane to communicate her thinking. She told her wife, "I love you. I am not going to interfere with how you parent your daughter. But because this house is mine as well, I am going to communicate my expectations to Annie if she is going to live here. If she fails to meet those expectations, I am not going to pretend they never existed. I will consider the next steps I'll need to take."

Donna followed through, telling Annie about her responsibilities as a member of the household. Because she had been working on building a relationship with Annie, Donna noticed that she felt less anxiety in defining these expectations. And I'd wager that Annie could sense that Donna was operating with a little more self. She'd probably noticed that her political lectures no longer baited Donna or caused her to shut down. Instead, she faced a more thoughtful stepmother, someone who was interested in their relationship, but unlikely to put up with a messy kitchen or unpaid rent.

Annie didn't magically become a responsible adult overnight. But she was able to do more than they'd assumed. By managing her anxiety in a more responsible way, Donna had taken some of the tension out of the system. In turn, everyone could think a little more clearly. Everyone was a little less influenced by relationship pressure. Annie eventually found a job with a local nonprofit, and she pitched in more around the house. She even started paying rent. The day she moved in with her communist boyfriend was a joyous day for all. Not just because Donna and Jane had the house to themselves, but also because all those ministeps had added up to something special. Donna knew she would have many future beers and conversations with her stepdaughter, and they could each keep being themselves.

And what about those raging neighbors? Donna didn't see her goal as convincing people to support the bike lane. It was simply to give herself the opportunity to show some emotional courage. She began telling people, "Yes, I think more bike lanes in our city is a good idea. I understand the challenges it creates, but ultimately I think the good outweighs the bad. What do you think?"

Working on differentiation doesn't mean that we shouldn't be angry at the injustices in the world, that we can't be fired up to make changes, right wrongs, and do good. It simply means that when we face great challenges, we can be more thoughtful about how we manage ourselves. You can direct your anxiety outward, becoming irresponsibly overinvolved in others' responses. You can respond with great immaturity, bullying others or hiding from the world's problems. Or you can define how you'd like to be a responsible self to others, and to the larger world. That only happens one small but courageous position at a time.

EXERCISE 1: **Look for the responders.** Look at your family, your workplace, or your larger community. Who are the reactors and who are the responders? We're all a necessary mix of both, but some people manage to pull off more of the latter. Consider how building relationships with the responders could be useful to you.

EXERCISE 2: **Sit-down time.** Choose one arena of life where you'd like to get some clarity on your own thinking. Maybe it's personal health, a political topic, a religious belief, or your principles for dating, work, or money. Can you write a page or two about your own beliefs? Can you be honest about what you're not sure you believe? Then consider what additional information, experiences, and conversations could help you develop your beliefs.

EXERCISE 3: **Mini-steps.** Courage requires deep thinking, but it also requires action. Can you be on the lookout for opportunities to define yourself to others? You don't have to stand on a table or chain yourself to the nearest nuclear waste site. Think about the small but important moments when we need to make decisions according to our best thinking. Maybe it's a one-on-one conversation after a tense exchange. Maybe it's saying no to a commitment you're not willing to make. Write down a few opportunities that might present themselves in the coming weeks.

- The emotional processes in the family also operate on a societal scale. You will see people and groups responding to stress in predictable patterns.
- One such pattern is the tendency to become irresponsibly overinvolved with other people. Bowen believed that a person who is working on being responsible for themselves will become more responsible toward others, without overfunctioning for them.
- A position is a step we take to be more responsibly involved with a challenge.
- When faced with local and global crises, we often choose reactions that are more about anxiety relief than engaging with problems.
- In order to stand up for our beliefs, we have to sit down and do the work of defining them. We have to let our beliefs be challenged by new information and experiences.
- Bowen described differentiation of self as a series of mini-steps, or positions we take based on our own thinking.

CONCLUSION

THE CHALLENGES WE FACE

"It only ends once. Anything that happens before that is just progress."

—Jacob, *Lost*

MORE THAN EVER, the world needs grown-ups. I do not presume to be any more mature than the next person. The more you learn about differentiation of self, the more you see the role of immaturity in your daily life. The more you realize how your actions often are more about keeping things calm than doing what's right. This is true in the family, and it's true in the broader world. We are just as likely to avoid global crises as we are to avoid Grandma. People will act out in the boardroom and at the dinner table. They will anxiously accommodate injustices, or abuses of power, as they would a screaming child. By sticking to what's automatic, we purchase stability at great cost.

I'd like to end the book by briefly discussing some of the bigger challenges we face, problems that require our best thinking, because I believe Bowen theory does offer a useful lens for these challenges. Harnessing our ability to act outside the bounds of a panicked, reptilian brain is exactly what makes us human. We can all find ways to build a more solid self, to be someone who has their operating instructions in front of them. By being true to our best thinking, we do become more responsible to others and our world.

WE'RE DISCONNECTED AND LONELY

The state of our relationships isn't strong. A quarter of Americans are currently cut off from a family member. Approximately twenty-five million people have experienced estrangement with a parent or child. There are certainly instances where ending contact is warranted, whether it's physical violence or other forms of abuse. But for many people, cutoff has simply been the family system's way of managing stress over the generations. There are people who'd like to bridge this gap but don't know how.

I do worry that the psychotherapy world, and its preoccupation with symptom relief, ignores the usefulness of systems thinking. When freedom from anxiety becomes the goal, rather than responsibility for self in relation to others, it's all too easy to drift away from person-to-person connections in the family. Perhaps learning to be ourselves, while connected to our family, has something to teach us yet. If only our insurance companies would cover such efforts!

We're also more disconnected from multigenerational relationships, both inside and outside the family. Millennials in particular are much less likely to have close intergenerational friendships. We are less connected to people in our neighborhood, in religious communities, or in other civic groups where you'll find generational diversity. If I could wave a wand and make my therapy clients do anything, I'd make them go out and get some friends who are much older and much younger than they are. It is a very modern phenomenon to be so isolated in our peer groups, and I worry we're worse off because of it.

We also know that the health risks associated with isolation are akin to smoking fifteen cigarettes a day. In a recent American survey, over one-third of adults reported feeling lonely much of the time. Half of young adults and mothers of little kids felt this way. Half the population would also like to have more meaningful relationships with our friends. How many of our maladies stem from this craving for more meaningful connection? In our efforts to individualize and medicalize everything, we have forgotten how social a species we are.

I hope you will leave this book with a kindled interest in building person-to-person relationships in your life. We become ourselves in relation to others, not in going it alone. Your family, your neighborhood, and the world benefit when you make the effort to connect in more authentic ways. We need people who connect with more self, people who are curious about the experiences and beliefs of others.

WE LIVE IN AN ANXIOUS, CHILD-FOCUSED SOCIETY

We're so worried about our kids. And we have plenty of reasons to be. Rates of anxiety, depression, and self-harm in teenagers have surged over the past decade. We're worried about gun violence, social media, and how the pandemic learning gap will affect younger generations. We're anxious about climate change, and what kind of world we'll leave our kids. But how much of our societal anxiety is managed through our intense focus on the next generation? I'd wager a lot. The cycle of child focus has never been more obvious as we desperately try to "fix" our kids.

In a recent Stanford study, researchers found that over-engagement in parents predicts poorer self-regulation in young children. The more a parent gave instructions, asked questions, or corrected their child during a task, the more the child struggled with managing themselves. Rather than blame modern parents for helicoptering, we can stop and see the reciprocity in this pattern. Are caregivers more likely to involve themselves if the kid is struggling? Probably. Are kids more likely to struggle if the adult is always swooping in and directing them? Sure.

Only the adult, however, has the capacity to hop off the Ferris wheel. We can find opportunities to let children operate without constant anxious intervention. Where they can build confidence in their own abilities, whether it's making friends, mastering tasks, or regulating their own emotions. Whether you're a parent or not, we can all work on building a world that promotes their resilience. We owe it to our kids to work on being more responsible for ourselves. Over the years, I've received many emails from parents wanting to send their twenty-five- or thirty-year-old to therapy. I always tell the parents that I'd be happy to work with *them* as they think about the challenges in this relationship.

Of course kids need resources. They need professionals and programs that can give them the support they need. But we also need more institutions, more programs that help adults work on themselves when children face challenges.

We need grown-ups who are not handing off their anxiety to the next generation.

WE'RE PERFORMING AND CONSUMING

We touch our phones more than 2,600 times a day. Very quickly, they have become a convenient way to manage our distress. When we're constantly switching between tasks, our brains and our relationships have little hope of reaching their potential.

The more we live our lives online, they more we become increasingly performative. Social media turns everyone into their own brand. If we're not careful, we lose our autonomy and originality, focusing on cultivating the image that will earn us the most approval. When you're competing with the entire world, you inevitably feel that you're not measuring up. We know that browsing on Instagram is associated with higher levels of negative body image. A majority of teen girls admit they feel sad and hopeless most of the time, and 30 percent admit they've seriously considered suicide. There may be more than social media at play here, but no one can deny its influence.

I also wonder what constant content consumption is doing to our minds. Silence is good for the brain, and mind wandering is essential for creativity. If we're forever scrolling or listening to content, we don't give ourselves time to absorb the information. We also don't give ourselves time to consider what we believe. We end up forever stuck in that game of *Supermarket Sweep*, snatching up the latest quick fix or popular belief.

What does it look like to make space in your day to know

your own mind? To evaluate yourself kindly, rather than scrolling for the quickest comparison? To do something not for the sake of the brand, but for your own passions or convictions? We need less consumption and performing, and more time for contemplation and connection. We need time to develop our best thinking and test it out in important relationships.

WE FACE COMPLEX PROBLEMS

If it feels like the world is speeding up, you're not wrong. Every year the news cycle gets faster, with topics landing and leaving before we can even educate ourselves. Blink and you'll miss the next natural disaster, mass shooting, political scandal, or rapid shift in artificial intelligence. Meanwhile the internet is elevating the angriest voices, making it all but impossible to cooperate to solve problems.

Despite all the chaotic chatter, there continue to be people who do slow, steady work. People who have managed to stay plugged in to complex problems over the long haul. People who can tolerate the discomfort that we can't quick-fix or rage-post our way out of any of these problems. Pay attention to these people. Consider the complex problems that draw your interest, and consider where you'd like to put your energy.

If you're looking for somewhere to start, let me suggest two things. First, keep learning about the natural world. Nothing calms me down more than reading about elephants or fungi or prairie voles. It helps me not be so hard on myself, and it keeps me fascinated by human behavior when I'm tempted to be judgmental. When we deny our connection to the natural world, to all living things, we disconnect ourselves from the power of evolution. And the human story is just getting started. Our unique capacity to learn, to watch and teach one another, is our greatest strength. If we've evolved our way into this mess, then perhaps we can evolve our way out of it. I say this as a person of faith, but also a person who sees, as Murray Bowen would say, that "the rats don't lie." We must bring the curiosity and delight of a researcher to our everyday challenges.

These challenges include our relationships, which brings me to my second suggestion. Join a group that is working on a challenge. We were not meant to solve problems in isolation. Denying the power of the group is denying what makes us human. So think about building relationships with people who are just as curious about a challenge. Whether it's creating a great school, a just world, or simply something beautiful.

My hope for you, and for myself, is that we live out the legacy of our humanity—the drives to connect with others and direct ourselves according to our beliefs. There has never been a better time for our very best thinking and our capacity to cooperate. We were built for both, and that is the delightful paradox of being a person in the world.

GROWING QUESTIONS

HERE IS A list of questions to help you thoughtfully engage with some of the ideas in the book. Some of them may apply to you, and some of them may not. But I'd encourage you to develop your own as you think about how to be more of a self in your relationships and challenges. A good question can do more than any anxious solution!

RELATIONSHIPS/MARRIAGE

- How much energy am I putting into making my partner what I want them to be? Into making myself what they want me to be?
- What would it look like to manage my own anxiety more effectively when my partner is distressed?
- When do I underfunction because I know my partner will take over?
- Am I able to listen to my partner talk about their challenges without overfunctioning for them?
- What are my principles for operating with maturity in the relationship?

FAMILY RELATIONSHIPS

- How does my family use distance or cutoff to manage tension?
- Where do I see opportunities for letting family members be more responsible for themselves? For being more responsible for myself in the family?
- How would I like to build stronger person-to-person relationships with family?
- What information can I gather that could help me be more objective about my family history and see relationship patterns?
- What wisdom would I like to hold on to when I visit with family?

FRIENDSHIPS

- How clumpy are my friend groups, and where do I see opportunities for building stronger person-to-person friendships?
- How much of my conversation with friends relies on superficial topics or gossip about others?
- When do I overfunction for friends so that I feel calmer and more in control?
- When have I failed to respect the individuality of my friends?
- When do I borrow self from friends (e.g. advice, reassurance, etc.) to manage my own anxiety?

PARENTING

- When have I been caught up in an anxious focus on my child/children?

- What parenting strategies have I borrowed from others without using my own thinking?
- Do I have guiding principles that describe how I want to function as a parent?
- How would I like to manage my own reactivity when my child is distressed?
- Am I able to discuss challenges with my child's other parent (or caregivers) while also giving them the space to develop their own thinking?

DATING

- What are my personal beliefs and principles for dating (e.g. dating maturely, safely, etc.)?
- Am I able to stay focused on being myself, instead of getting people to like me?
- Am I able to thoughtfully manage how and how often I use dating apps?
- How can I access my own thinking before asking friends for advice?
- How would I like to manage my distress when a person doesn't text or call back?

WORK

- How can I strengthen my own ability to evaluate myself at work, rather than always relying on feedback or praise from others?
- What relationship patterns do I see at work (i.e. triangles), and what has been my part in them?
- With whom at work do I need to work on developing a stronger person-to-person relationship?

- How do I overfunction or underfunction at work when I am distressed?
- Do I have a realistic definition of what good work or a productive day looks like?

BELIEFS AND PRINCIPLES

- In what areas of life am I operating with more pseudo-self, anxiously adopting or abandoning beliefs because of relationship pressure?
- Where have I been able to operate with more solid self?
- In what areas of life would I like to spend time developing my beliefs?
- How do I respond when I encounter information that challenges my beliefs?
- What would it look like to define my thinking to others without trying to convince or control them?

CONTENT CONSUMPTION

- When do I consume content to manage my own anxiety or boost my mood?
- How can I make time to develop my own thinking, or let my mind wander?
- When have I borrowed advice from experts without using my own thinking?
- What would it look like to engage with the internet, my phone, etc., more thoughtfully?
- Have I developed guiding principles for how I want to use social media?

WORKING ON GOALS

- What are the ways I'd like to be more responsible for myself in my day-to-day life?
- How do I borrow unrealistic or unhelpful definitions of health, beauty, success, etc., from the culture?
- What does it look like to be flexible, creative, and kind to myself when one approach to a goal doesn't work for me?
- How can I develop my own thinking when I'm relying too much on praise or encouragement from others?
- How can I stay focused on myself, without needing others to adopt my goals or function the way I function?

MENTAL, PHYSICAL, EMOTIONAL HEALTH

- Do I have clear beliefs and principles about how I want to care for my body and mind?
- What does it look like when I'm managing anxiety irresponsibly? More responsibly?
- How would I like to be more responsibly involved with my work with my doctor, therapist, etc.?
- Am I able to talk about my challenges without trying to be responsible for people's anxious reactions to them?
- How can I stay curious about my challenges without shaming or blaming myself?

LOCAL AND GLOBAL CHALLENGES

- What does it look like to be responsibly connected to my community (e.g. neighborhood, religious congregation, volunteer organization)?
- What does it look like to be responsibly connected to national or global challenges?
- Who are the people in my community who have been able to stay thoughtfully engaged with complex problems?
- When have my reactions to hard things been more about calming myself down than responding with my best thinking?
- How can I define my thinking about complex problems without trying to control others?

BOWEN THEORY RESOURCES

IF YOU'D LIKE to read more of my writing about Bowen theory, you can subscribe to my free newsletter, theanxiousover achiever.substack.com. You can also visit thebowencenter.org to learn about the Bowen Center for the Study of the Family, a nonprofit founded by Murray Bowen that offers training programs for the theory. There are many such centers in the United States and around the globe who can connect you to training programs or therapists who use Bowen theory.

I'd also recommend these books to continue learning about the theory:

Brown, Jenny. *Growing Yourself Up: How to Bring Your Best to All of Life's Relationships*. Wollombi, New South Wales, Australia: Exisle, 2012.

Harrison, Victoria. *The Family Diagram & Family Research: An Illustrated Guide to Tools for Working on Differentiation of Self in One's Family*. Center for the Study of Natural Systems and the Family, 2018.

Kerr, Michael E. *Bowen Theory's Secrets: Revealing the Hidden Life of Families*. New York: Norton, 2019.

Kerr, Michael E. *One Family's Story: A Primer on Bowen Theory*. Georgetown Family Center, 2017.

ACKNOWLEDGMENTS

This book would not have been possible without the individuality of many smart, kind, and capable people.

I am grateful to Murray Bowen for his thinking, determination, and legacy.

The many people who have dedicated their professional lives to teaching, researching, and writing about Bowen theory.

The faculty of the Bowen Center, for the gift of working with people who are working on differentiation of self.

Jessica Felleman, for her guidance, smarts, and patience, and for being an all-around fantastic human.

Sallie Lotz, for giving me a chance to write about Bowen theory and helping me connect these ideas to today's challenges.

Thank you to the teams at St. Martin's Essentials and Jennifer Lyons Literary Agency for their creativity and dedication to this project.

Thank you to my newsletter readers for all your kind words and support. To members of the Heim family for encouragement and essential childcare. To members of Capitol Hill United Methodist Church for giving me countless examples of people who stay plugged in to complex problems. To my own family, the emotional system with whom I'm proud to dance.

Thanks to Jacob for always betting on me. And thanks to my daughter, who likes to say, "Focus on yourself, Mommy." I'm working on it.

NOTES

INTRODUCTION

p. 4: **In the 1950s, Bowen led** . . . Bowen, M., & Butler, J. (2015). *The Origins of Family Psychotherapy: The NIMH Family Study Project.* Lanham, MD: Rowman & Littlefield Publishers.

p. 6: **Bowen also observed** . . . Bowen, M. (1978). *Family Therapy in Clinical Practice.* New York: Aronson.

2. THE COST OF KEEPING PEOPLE HAPPY

p. 32: **Psychologists sometimes call it** . . . Striano, T., & Rochat, P. (1999). "Developmental Link Between Dyadic and Triadic Social Competence in Infancy," *British Journal of Developmental Psychology,* 17(4), 551–562.

3. HOW WE END UP BORROWING OUR BELIEFS

p. 54: **A cockroach community** . . . Ward, A. (2022). *The Social Lives of Animals.* New York: Basic Books.

p. 54: **In one famous study** . . . Hopper, L. M., Schapiro, S. J., Lambeth, S. P., & Brosnan, S. F. (2011). "Chimpanzees' Socially Maintained Food Preferences Indicate Both Conservatism and Conformity," *Animal Behaviour,* 81(6), 1195–1202.

p. 54: **"It takes less than . . ."** Sapolsky, R. M. (2017). *Behave: The Biology of Humans at Our Best and Worst.* New York: Penguin Books.

p. 60: **Around the time you were born** . . . Spreng, R. N., & Andrews-Hanna, J. R. (2015). "The Default Network and Social Cognition," Elsevier eBooks, 165–169.

p. 61: "The great gift . . ." Wilson, D. S. (2020). *This View of Life: Completing the Darwinian Revolution*. New York: Vintage Books.

4. HOW WE END UP OVERFUNCTIONING
FOR OTHERS

p. 68: A dog's levels . . . Yong, M. H., & Ruffman, T. (2014). "Emotional Contagion: Dogs and Humans Show a Similar Physiological Response to Human Infant Crying," *Behavioural Processes*, 108, 155–165.

5. HOW WE END UP UNDERFUNCTIONING

p. 93: In one fascinating study . . . Carr, P. B., & Walton, G. M. (2014). "Cues of Working Together Fuel Intrinsic Motivation," *Journal of Experimental Social Psychology*, 53, 169–184.
p. 98: Your brain can get a nice dose . . . Rice, M. E. (2019). "Closing in on What Motivates Motivation," *Nature*, 570 (7759), 40–42.
p. 103: In her book about Bowen theory . . . Gilbert, R. M. (2017). *Extraordinary Relationships: A New Way of Thinking About Human Interactions*. Leading Systems Press.

6. THE WAYS WE DISTANCE FROM OTHERS

p. 114: He outlined three key qualities . . . Bowen, M. (1978). *Family Therapy in Clinical Practice*. New York: Aronson.
p. 115: In a more open relationship system . . . Papero, D. (2018). "Developing a Systems Model for Family Assessment," *Family Systems: A Journal of Natural Systems Thinking in Psychiatry and the Sciences*, 13(2).

7. HOW WE END UP BLAMING OTHERS

p. 131: A female chimpanzee . . . De Waal, F. (2007). *Chimpanzee Politics: Power and Sex Among Apes*. Baltimore, MD: Johns Hopkins University Press.

p. 140: Dave and Cindy were stuck . . . Brown, J. (2023) "Making Sense of the Parenting 'Soft/Hard Split,'" *Australian and New Zealand Journal of Family Therapy*, 44, 225–236.

8. ENDING THE CHASE FOR APPROVAL AND ATTENTION

p. 155: Researchers have observed that people will mimic . . . Gregory, S. W., & Webster, S. (1996). "A Nonverbal Signal in Voices of Interview Partners Effectively Predicts Communication Accommodation and Social Status Perceptions," *Journal of Personality and Social Psychology*, 70(6), 1231–1240.

p. 155: Small children will notice . . . Chudek, M., Heller, S., Birch, S., & Henrich, J. (2012). "Prestige-Biased Cultural Learning: Bystanders' Differential Attention to Potential Models Influences Children's Learning," *Evolution and Human Behavior*, 33(1), 46–56.

p. 158: More dopamine is released . . . Sapolsky, R. M. (2017). *Behave: The Biology of Humans at Our Best and Worst*. New York: Penguin Books.

p. 158: Put a mirror in front of someone . . . Beaman, A. L., Klentz, B., Diener, E., & Svanum, S. (1979). "Self-Awareness and Transgression in Children: Two Field Studies," *Journal of Personality and Social Psychology*, 37(10), 1835–1846.

p. 158: or a set of cartoon eyes . . . Ernest-Jones, M., Nettle, D., & Bateson, M. (2011). "Effects of Eye Images on Everyday Cooperative Behavior: A Field Experiment," *Evolution and Human Behavior*, 32(3), 172–178.

p. 162: In his book *Bowen Theory's Secrets* . . . Kerr, M. E. (2019). *Bowen Theory's Secrets: Revealing the Hidden Life of Families*. New York: Norton.

10. BECOMING MORE RESPONSIBLE FOR OURSELVES

p. 188: Put a rhesus monkey . . . Sapolsky, R. M. (2017). *Behave: The Biology of Humans at Our Best and Worst*. New York: Penguin Books.

p. 188: Differences in the volume . . . Powell, J., Lewis, P. A., Roberts, N., García-Fiñana, M., & Dunbar, R. I. M. (2012). "Orbital Prefrontal Cortex Volume Predicts Social Network Size: An Imaging Study of Individual Differences in Humans," *Proceedings of the Royal Society B: Biological Sciences*, 279(1736), 2157–2162.

p. 188: Outlasting our less social Neanderthal cousins . . . Pearce, E., Stringer, C., & Dunbar, R. I. M. (2013). "New Insights into Differences in Brain Organization Between Neanderthals and Anatomically Modern Humans," *Proceedings of the Royal Society B: Biological Sciences*, 280(1758), 2130–2140.

p. 196: Somewhere in this process . . . Ngo, L., Kelly, M., Coutlee, C. G., Carter, R. M., Sinnott-Armstrong, W., & Huettel, S. A. (2015). "Two Distinct Moral Mechanisms for Ascribing and Denying Intentionality," *Scientific Reports*, 5(1).

11. BUILDING STRONGER RELATIONSHIPS

p. 208: Baby rhesus monkeys . . . Harlow, H. F., Dodsworth, R. O., & Harlow, M. K. (1965). "Total Social Isolation in Monkeys," *Proceedings of the National Academy of Sciences*, 54(1), 90–97.

p. 208: Cows will lick . . . Laister, S., Stockinger, B., Regner, A.-M., Zenger, K., Knierim, U., & Winckler, C. (2011). "Social Licking in Dairy Cattle—Effects on Heart Rate in Performers and Receivers," *Applied Animal Behaviour Science*, 130(3–4), 81–90.

12. LEARNING TO EVALUATE OURSELVES

p. 225: In Western cultures . . . Spiegel, A. (October 6, 2007). "Americans Flunk Self-Assessment," *All Things Considered*, NPR. Radio broadcast transcript. https://www.npr.org/templates/story/story.php?storyId=15073430.

13. FINDING THE COURAGE TO TAKE A POSITION

p. 244: Bowen wrote . . . Bowen, M. (1978). *Family Therapy in Clinical Practice*. New York: Aronson.

CONCLUSION

p. 257: Approximately twenty-five million people . . . Pillemer, K. (2022). *Fault Lines.* New York: Penguin.

p. 257: Millennials in particular . . . Levy, V., & Thayer, C. (2020). "The Positive Impact of Intergenerational Friendships." AARP. https://www.aarp.org/research/topics/life/info-2019 /friendship-across-the-ages.html.

p. 258: We also know that the health risks . . . Holt-Lunstad, J., Smith, T. B., Baker, M., Harris, T., & Stephenson, D. (2015). "Loneliness and Social Isolation as Risk Factors for Mortality," *Perspectives on Psychological Science,* 10(2), 227–237. https://doi .org/10.1177/1745691614568352.

p. 258: In a recent American survey . . . Weissbourd, R., Batanova, M., Lovison, V., & Torres, E. (February 2021). "Loneliness in America: How the Pandemic Has Deepened an Epidemic of Loneliness and What We Can Do About It." Making Caring Common Project. https://mcc.gse.harvard.edu/reports /loneliness-in-america.

p. 259: In a recent Stanford study . . . Obradović, J., Sulik, M. J., & Shaffer, A. (2021). "Learning to Let Go: Parental Over-Engagement Predicts Poorer Self-Regulation in Kindergartners," *Journal of Family Psychology,* 35(8). https://doi.org/10.1037 /fam0000838.

p. 260: We touch our phones . . . Winnick, M., & Zolna R. (2016). "Putting a Finger on Our Phone Obsession." Dscout.com. https: //dscout.com/people-nerds/mobile-touches.

p. 260: We know that browsing on Instagram . . . Alfonso-Fuertes, I., Alvarez-Mon, M. A., Sanchez Del Hoyo, R., Ortega, M. A., Alvarez-Mon, M., & Molina-Ruiz, R. M. (2023). "Time Spent on Instagram and Body Image, Self-esteem, and Physical Comparison Among Young Adults in Spain: Observational Study," *JMIR formative research,* 7, e42207.

p. 260: A majority of teen girls . . . CDC. (February 13, 2023). "U.S. Teen Girls Experiencing Increased Sadness and Violence." Centers for Disease Control and Prevention. https://www.cdc .gov/media/releases/2023/p0213-yrbs.html.